Legal Affairs of the
Khul'u

Al-Rahmaniyyah Press
Camden, NJ

1st Edition 1444AH / March 2022CE

Published by:
Al-Rahmaniyyah Press
PO Box 8671
Turnersville, NJ
08012-9997
U.S.A.
Electronic mail: editor@alrahmaniyyah.com
ISBN: 9798424340208

Cover design: Al-Rahmaniyyah Press

Legal Affairs of the

Khul'u

Containing issues related to healthy marital relations, marital discord, appointing the two referees, and the *khul'u*, including its evidence from the Book, the Sunnah and statements of the foremost scholars

By Dr. Taqi al-Deen al-Hilali

Translated by Tariq Ben Nuriddin Porter

About the Author

He was the magnificent scholar, the Muhaddith (scholar of hadith), the famous linguist and brilliant scholar of literature, the extraordinary poet and great Moroccan traveler of great distances [seeking knowledge], the Shaikh Muhammad al-Taqi, better known as Muhammad Taqi al-Deen. He was born in 1311 Hijri, which coincides with the Gregorian year of 1894. He studied the Qur'an with his father and memorized it by the age of 12.

Most of us in the West may have first encountered his name on the cover of the well-known translation of the Qur'an entitled, *The Noble Qur'an*. He was instrumental in that work from which most of us have benefited tremendously. That said, this brilliant Moroccan scholar was much more than a translator who spoke various languages fluently, including English, Spanish, German, and French. Shaikh Muhammad spent his life in the path of seeking knowledge and spreading the correct teachings of Islam, the call [and way] of the Salaf (the exemplary Muslims of early Islamic history). From among his countless trips seeking knowledge, after having performed hajj, he traveled to India to gain knowledge in a field of study that he so desired to reach his potential in, the science of Hadith. He met with various major scholars there where he both imparted knowledge and learned. Among the greatest of those scholars that he met with was the grand scholar of hadith, the Shaikh Abd al-Rahman ibn Abd al-Rahim al-Mubarakfuri, the author of "Tuhfa al-Ahwathi an Explanation of Jami' al-Tirmithi. He learned the science of hadith from

Shaikh al-Mubarakfuri and the Shaikh gave him ijaza[1]. Shaikh Muhammad Taqi al-Deen praised Shaikh al-Mubarakfuri in a poem in which he urged students of knowledge to hold dearly to [the science and knowledge of] hadith and to the aforementioned explanation [of Shaikh al-Mubarakfuri]. This poem was included in the fourth edition of the Indian print of the book. Likewise, he also resided with Shaikh Muhammad ibn Hussain ibn Muhsin al-Hadidi al-Ansari al-Yamani (the Yemeni) who was living in India at the time. He read portions of the Kutub al-Sittah (the six foremost collections of hadith) and this Shaikh also gave him ijaza. The Shaikh traveled and his journey upon the path of learning and teaching was tremendous and vast.

It is noteworthy to mention here the fact that the Shaikh was a follower of the Tijaniyyah Sufi order in the early part of his life yet learned of their misguidance and turned to the way of Ahl al-Sunnah (the group of Muslims who adhere to the way and teachings of Prophet Muhammad). Shaikh Abd al-Aziz ibn Baz said about him in his book, "Tuhfa al-Ikhwan bi Tarajum b'adh al-A'yan" on pg. 70, "... and he has many books, of them "Al-Hadiyyah al-Hadiyah Li al-Firqah al-Tijaniyyah". In the early part of his life, he was Tijani. Then, Allah ridded him of that [misguided] way [by guiding him to the way of the Salaf]. Thereafter, he refuted the people of the Tijaniyyah sect, uncovering their grave errors." In 1968 Gregorian, he received an invitation from the Honorable

---

[1] *Ijaza* is the traditional Islamic system by which a teacher vouches and certifies that his student has studied and thoroughly grasped specific lessons or knowledge from him (i.e. Qur'an, hadith, etc.).

Shaikh Abd al-Aziz ibn Baz, the President of the Islamic University of Madinah al-Munawwara at the time, to work as a part-time professor [allowing that he travel back and forth] from Morocco. He accepted the offer and continued working there until 1974 when he decided to leave the university and return to Meknes in Morocco to dedicate his complete focus on calling to the way of Allah. Hence, he began teaching in mosques and traveling throughout Morocco spreading the call [and way] of the Salaf.

Shaikh Muhammad Taqi al-Deen died on the 25th of Shawwal, 1407 Hijri, coinciding with the 22nd of June 1987. He passed away in his home in Casablanca, Morocco.

May Allah have mercy on him and allow his knowledge and work to continue to benefit Muslims and the entire world.

Contents

Translator's Introduction

All praise is due to Allah, the Lord of all worlds. I pray that His most special blessings be upon the greatest of His creation, His final Prophet and Messenger, Muhammad ibn Abdullah.

It is an honor to present to readers this translation of one of the numerous precious works of an eminent scholar of Islam of the twentieth century, the Shaykh Muhammad Taqi al-Deen al-Hilali. This book is yet another attestation to not only his genius but, more importantly, to the broad scope of Islamic law and the great attention it gives to the rights of women. The religion of Islam is a comprehensive and complete way of life, in a way in which those who do not truly know it cannot really appreciate. The justice and balance taught in the Qur'an and Sunnah cover one's personal life and dealings, as well as every aspect of one's social life. While Islam teaches that men and women are equal with regards to their essence, their spiritual potential and their opportunity to reach the highest levels of success in this life and in Paradise, it does still necessarily address circumstances and affairs which are specific to men, and in other instances those which are specific to women.

Contrary to what many who are ignorant about Islam may believe, women have full right to end their marriage when they truly feel that is best for them. Under the laws of Islam, they are never trapped in a marriage with a man they do not love, or even like for that matter. The author clarifies that a woman's displeasure with her husband may be due to physical characteristics or character flaws. This book details the rules, conditions and circumstances of this type of divorce in Islam. It is called a *khul'ah* when referring to a singular occurrence, while *khul'u* is the broader form of the term used to refer to this type of divorce more generally. Moreover, the author sheds light on the meaning and context of several verses in the Qur'an that are often misconstrued and taken out of context by those with ulterior motives and biased agendas against this amazing religion.

One such issue is the "hitting" mentioned in the Qur'an permitting a husband to lightly hit his wife in very dire and particular circumstances. Firstly, it is important we emphasize that it is absolutely prohibited in Islam to hit anyone, even animals, in the face. Further, the Prophet taught that true strength is not with force but controlling oneself when angry. Therefore, the light, harmless hit referred to here is only allowed when a man believes that his wife will respond positively to this gesture. It is intended as an expression of a husband's complete displeasure with his wife's transgression upon his rights as a husband. The author makes it crystal clear that this light hit allowed in Islam under very specific circumstances, which based on the description of foremost scholars is clearly more like a tap, is meant to express that the husband has reached his limit in patience with his wife's obstinate mistreatment, and is not for any other reason. Further, this light hit, which the Prophet Muhammad clarified must not cause pain, should only be done if the wife has committed serious transgression against the husband, and only if the husband truly believes that his wife will respond positively to this expression of his displeasure. Shaikh Taqi al-Deen says, "We understand from this that if a woman does commit one of these [unacceptable] acts, and her man has hope that their relationship can be rectified; and he believes that in hitting her lightly in a manner which does not hurt, as detailed above, their relationship could possibly return to a good and healthy state, it is permitted for him to hit her [lightly] with the intention of rectifying their marriage ~ not with the intention of getting revenge." This is only one example of how the author sheds light on aspects of Islamic law that even some Muslims have gravely misunderstood and transgressed boundaries due to their culture, whims and misguidance.

Readers, both Muslim and non-Muslim, are bound to discover details and jewels about the *khul'u*, and the rights and honorable status of women in Islam in general, which they were not aware of. This book brilliantly showcases the true empowerment of women given by Allah ~ the Creator of all ~ established as law in Islam over fourteen hundred years ago. Any individual or group of people who oppose the guidance of the Qur'an and *Sunnah* in their treatment of women, or in any other action or behavior involving oppression of others and extremism, represent themselves while Islam is far removed from all misguidance, oppression and injustice.

I would like to thank my close friend, Abu al-Hasan Malik al-Akhdar, for his recommendation that I translate this precious work. His consistent support as well as his persistent encouragement played an essential role throughout the process. I would also like to thank Umm Abdullah for editing the book and offering very valuable feedback and recommendations.

I hope and pray that this book benefits all who read it and, through them, those whose lives they impact.

Written by
Tariq Ben Nuriddin Porter
August 19, 2021
Casablanca, Morocco

Author's Introduction

In the name of Allah, The Most Gracious, The Most Merciful

All praise is due to Allah; He revealed the Clear Book (the Qur'an) to his servant (Muhammad). He sent him as a mercy to all worlds (i.e. all creation), to help those oppressed and to return the rights of those who are deprived to them, to make people's rights and obligations equal. Oh Allah, grant your special blessings and peace to him, and to his companions and those who follow him til the Day of Judgement.

That said, I have noticed that people in our country and elsewhere, without doubt, have seriously oppressed women. A minority of men nowadays refrain from transgressing upon the rights of women and mistreating them. In turn, wives have responded with similar treatment (towards their husbands). As a result, these affairs have become terrible in public and in private, causing widespread marital turmoil and absence of cooperation. Each spouse has become a heavy burden on the other. *Shari'ah*[2] courts have become overwhelmed with disputes, and judges have not been able to solve the problems of the people.

---

[2] T.N.: *Shari'ah* is Islamic law

This is all due to the deviation [of our people] from the path of the *Book*[3] and the *Sunnah*[4]. People have taken to wandering blindly in darkness like one with no knowledge or vision. And since men are (physically) strong and women are (physically) weak [when compared to most men], injustice has been occurring in legal rulings, and judges have implemented rulings which their enemies, [from among] the Europeans, consider discrimination and depriving women of their rights, thereby distorting the beauty of this pure, upright *Shari'ah* and causing each gender to transgress the legal boundaries set by Allah. Due to this, sincerity between husband and wife has vanished and unhappiness and argumentation have overcome each group [husbands and wives].

I, therefore, see it incumbent upon myself to write a work small in size yet full of knowledge which will bring justice for those who have been oppressed, to uncover [and bring to light] the rights of those who have had them wrongfully taken; so that each spouse knows what Allah has made mandatory upon him or her and so that harsh character is replaced by manners of the highest standard. This is in order to prepare them for a splendid marital companionship and a peaceful home. For everyone who reads it and implements the wise Qur'anic verses, and the noble Prophetic *Sunnah* which it consists of, the gates of happiness will open, and - God willing - they will attain the great reward of paradise and the additional reward [which Allah has promised believers]. This applies to rulers

---

[3] T.N.: The Qur'an

[4] T.N.: The prophetic guidance, way of life and tradition

and laymen. I have named this work "The Legal Affairs of The *Khul'u* in Islam".

Furthermore, I ask Allah to make it a benefit for whomever He wills of His slaves (His creation) and bless me to have written it solely for his sake; and that He makes it a means of attaining the blissful gardens of Paradise. I have begun this work in response to the request of scholars that the issue at hand be addressed.

Lastly, once I had completed the book and read it for a second time, it dawned upon me to add footnotes in order to [further] clarify a few topics and add completion to others. I have therefore added them, and they are a quarter of the length of the book itself. They contain points of benefit and additional information which I hope serve to add more value towards realizing the outcome for which the book has been written. And Allah is the One for whom we strive.

Written by Muhammed Taqi ul-Deen al-Hilali in the Prophetic City (Madinah) on 13 Rabi' al-Thani 1390 AH.

The Honorable Status of Women in Islam

Allah says in chapter al-Nisa verse 35,

وَإِنْ خِفْتُمْ شِقَاقَ بَيْنِهِمَا فَٱبْعَثُواْ حَكَمًا مِّنْ أَهْلِهِ، وَحَكَمًا مِّنْ أَهْلِهَآ إِن يُرِيدَآ إِصْلَٰحًا يُوَفِّقِ ٱللَّهُ بَيْنَهُمَآ إِنَّ ٱللَّهَ كَانَ عَلِيمًا خَبِيرًا ۝

> "And if you fear strife between them (the
> husband and wife), appoint a judge from his
> people and one from hers. As long as they
> truly seek to resolve the problem, Allah will
> guide them to success [in solving their issues].
> Indeed Allah is All-Knowing and All-Aware."
> [Chapter al-Nisa: 4:35]

What does one with deep understanding comprehend from
this verse; he (or she) understands that a woman is not cattle
nor is she some sort of property which is bought, with which
an "owner" can do whatever he pleases. Likewise, she is not
void of the right to oppose her husband, or to defend her
rights, or raise her complaints to a judge. If he, then, gives her
her rights, implementing the compassion that even an animal
deserves, he succeeds and is guided aright; if he transgresses
upon her rights, the account of all that he has done will be
settled by Allah.

Concerning the wife, she is an honored human being of
intellect, included in the statement of Allah,

$$\{ \ast \ \text{وَلَقَدْ كَرَّمْنَا بَنِي آدَمَ وَحَمَلْنَاهُمْ فِي ٱلْبَرِّ وَٱلْبَحْرِ وَرَزَقْنَاهُم مِّنَ} \}$$

$$\{ \text{ٱلطَّيِّبَاتِ وَفَضَّلْنَاهُمْ عَلَىٰ كَثِيرٍ مِّمَّنْ خَلَقْنَا تَفْضِيلًا} \ ⑦ \}$$

"Indeed, We have honored the children of Adam and have carried them by land and by sea. Likewise, We have surely provided them with the best of provision, and We raised them in excellence over much of that which We have created in a tremendous way."
[Chapter Al-Isra: 70].

Allah honored the offspring of Adam, men and women, with an attractive appearance and with the intellect by way of which He has made everything in this world subjected to him (human beings). He has placed them in the position of leadership and control over other creatures and creation like animals, plants and inanimate objects. Furthermore, he honored them with the abilities of speech, complex thinking and carrying the responsibility for which they will ultimately enjoy the everlasting life of pleasure and happiness, never to die again ~ those whom Allah wills to attain it.

These special characteristics are spread among men and women. Therefore, whoever treats his wife like an animal or a piece of property, in legal affairs or in general dealings, then indeed he has withheld the blessing of Allah [which is due to her], and he deserves that Allah enables outsiders and others who will conquer him and treat him in the same manner; "Howsoever you treat others, so shall you be treated." The *nun* (Arabic letter) is omitted [in this proverb], yet not due to a *nasib* or a *jazim* (two Arabic grammatical forms). This is just as is found in the statement of the Prophet (may Allah's most special blessings and peace be upon him) "You will not enter paradise unless you believe, and you will not truly believe until you love one another; shall I inform you of an action which, if you do it, you will come to love one another, spread the greetings of peace amongst you."

أبيت أسري و تبيتي ندلكي   شعرك بالعمبر و المسك الذكي

I sleep the night away as you spend your night,
massaging your hair with amber and musk

Herein, the *nun*[5] is omitted from the words تبيتي and تدلكي and it is *nasib*[6] and not *jazim*[7], which is a rare case.

Furthermore, the Most-High says in chapter *al-Baqarah*,

﴿ وَلَهُنَّ مِثْلُ ٱلَّذِى عَلَيْهِنَّ بِٱلْمَعْرُوفِ ۚ ٢٢٨ ﴾

---

[5] T.N.: A letter of the Arabic alphabet which makes the sound of the English letter 'n'.

[6] T.N.: An Arabic grammatical case which involves altering verbs in particular ways depending on the verb's position and role in a sentence or phrase. It is often characterized by the *fatha* at the end of simple verbs. Often times particular letters are omitted in such word alterations.

[7] T.N.: An Arabic grammatical case which involves altering verbs in particular ways due depending on the verb's position and role in a sentence or phrase. It is often characterized by the *sukoon* at the end of simple verbs.

"And just as they (women) are responsible for rendering rights to their husbands, they possess similar rights over them." [al-Baqarah: 228]

Allah has granted rights which must be upheld to everyone, and it is not permissible to deprive anyone of their rights. Furthermore, the position in which Allah has placed men is to bear the burden of leading, which concerns financial care as well as [overall] protection. This does not mean [or give license to] oppressing, transgressing, victimizing or impeding upon the rights [of others]. Allah says in chapter al-Nisa, verse 32,

$$﴿ لِّلرِّجَالِ نَصِيبٌ مِّمَّا ٱكْتَسَبُواْ وَلِلنِّسَآءِ نَصِيبٌ مِّمَّا ٱكْتَسَبْنَ ۚ ٣٢ ﴾$$

"Men will be rewarded based on what they have earned and likewise women will be rewarded based on what they have earned." [al-Nisa: 4:32]

Imams Ahmed and al-Tirmithi reported that the incident for which this verse was revealed (sabab ul-nuzool) is in a narration of the Mother-of-the-Believers, Umm Salamah, when she said, "Oh Messenger of Allah! Men fight in battle and so do we, yet we receive only half [of what men receive] from inheritance. Thereby, Allah sent down the verse,

$$﴿ وَلَا تَتَمَنَّوْاْ مَا فَضَّلَ ٱللَّهُ بِهِۦ بَعْضَكُمْ عَلَىٰ بَعْضٍ ۚ ٣٢ ﴾$$

"And do not have envy concerning that with which We have blessed some and not others." [al-Nisa: 4:32]

Ibn Abee Hatim also reported this, as well as Ibn Jarir, and al-Hakim in his *Mustadrak* – with different wordings yet a unified meaning.

Concerning Allah's statement towards the end of chapter Ali Imran,

﴿ فَٱسْتَجَابَ لَهُمْ رَبُّهُمْ أَنِّي لَآ أُضِيعُ عَمَلَ عَٰمِلٍ مِّنكُم مِّن ذَكَرٍ أَوْ أُنثَىٰ بَعْضُكُم مِّنۢ بَعْضٍ ۖ ١٩٥ ﴾

"So, their Lord responded to them saying, 'Indeed, I never neglect the good deeds of any of you, be you men or women.'" [*Aali Imran*: 3:195]

Saeed bin Mansour reported, with his chain of narrators to Umm Salamah, that she said, "Oh Messenger of Allah, we haven't heard Allah mention anything about women concerning the *hijrah* (migration from Makkah to Madinah). Thereby, Allah sent down, "So, their Lord responded to them..." to the end of the verse (above). And the Most-High says in chapter al-Ahzab, verse 35,

﴿ إِنَّ ٱلْمُسْلِمِينَ وَٱلْمُسْلِمَٰتِ وَٱلْمُؤْمِنِينَ وَٱلْمُؤْمِنَٰتِ وَٱلْقَٰنِتِينَ وَٱلْقَٰنِتَٰتِ وَٱلصَّٰدِقِينَ وَٱلصَّٰدِقَٰتِ وَٱلصَّٰبِرِينَ وَٱلصَّٰبِرَٰتِ وَٱلْخَٰشِعِينَ وَٱلْخَٰشِعَٰتِ وَٱلْمُتَصَدِّقِينَ وَٱلْمُتَصَدِّقَٰتِ وَٱلصَّٰٓئِمِينَ وَٱلصَّٰٓئِمَٰتِ وَٱلْحَٰفِظِينَ فُرُوجَهُمْ وَٱلْحَٰفِظَٰتِ وَٱلذَّٰكِرِينَ ٱللَّهَ كَثِيرًا وَٱلذَّٰكِرَٰتِ أَعَدَّ ٱللَّهُ لَهُم مَّغْفِرَةً وَأَجْرًا عَظِيمًا ٣٥ ﴾

"Indeed, Muslim men and women, believing men and women, men and women who call on Him in supplication, truthful men and women, men and women who have tremendous awareness and fear of

Allah, men and women who give charity, fasting men and women, chaste men and women, men and women who remember Allah often; Allah has prepared forgiveness for them and a tremendous reward."
[Al-Ahzab: 33:35]

Allah, highly exalted above all imperfections, mentions herein ten attributes of His believers because of which He has made His forgiveness and a tremendous reward mandatory for whosoever lives up to them, be they men or women. The Most-High says in chapter al-Nahl, verse 97,

$$ \text{﴿ مَنْ عَمِلَ صَٰلِحًا مِّن ذَكَرٍ أَوْ أُنثَىٰ وَهُوَ مُؤْمِنٌ فَلَنُحْيِيَنَّهُۥ حَيَوٰةً طَيِّبَةً وَلَنَجْزِيَنَّهُمْ أَجْرَهُم بِأَحْسَنِ مَا كَانُوا۟ يَعْمَلُونَ ٩٧ ﴾} $$

"Whoever does good deeds, be they men or women, and is a believer, We will grant him [or her] a good life, and We will grant reward to them according to the best of what they used to do."
[al-Nahl: 16:97]

Allah promises men and women that for whoever amongst them does good deeds, He will grant them a great life in this world and reward them in the hereafter with the most tremendous of rewards. So, when a man treats his wife as he treats his grazing animal, what type of "good life" is that for her? Furthermore, he who treats his wife badly and claims it is his right is [in actuality] a denier of the Qur'an [and its teachings]. And we as Muslims ask Allah to grant us success in following the *Book* and the *Sunnah* of the Messenger (may the most special blessing of Allah and peace be upon him), as well as in implementation of the *Shari'ah*. So, we do not say as the Europeans say in their extremism and their patronizing [claim] that women are the better half of men.[8] Moreover, this

---

[8] I expounded upon this somewhat in the article "Traditional Education of Females" in which I included various incidents that I personally witnessed in Europe. I used these [incidents] as proof for what I mentioned concerning the European's deception of women and their harshness towards them. I add to this that the English Muslim professor, Marmaduke Pickthall, who translated the noble Qur'an, authored books in support of Islam and the Excellence of the Arabs who spread Islam. He said in his book "The Excellence of Arabs", "Indeed, Muslims revere the woman and honor her because she's a woman. We see that they take care of the needs of widows, not leaving them with the necessity to have to buy the things they need at a market. They honor their mothers to the extent that some of them even obey their mothers as an obedient servant obeys his master, holding her as the master of the home, the overall ruler of the home as well as with his wife, children and grandchildren. Moreover, we have witnessed businessmen and wealthy men who do not buy a home or land except after consulting their mothers and ensuring that she's pleased [with making the purchase]. We have likewise witnessed them [Muslims] demonstrating compassion with every weak [or disadvantaged] woman, due to old age, or loss of relatives, or [even] bad looks; they serve them for the Face of Allah, seeking His pleasure.

As for Europeans, they only revere women when two conditions are met: one is that she be beautiful in their eyes; two is that she dresses in a manner which exposes her beauty allowing others the enjoyment [of looking at her]. Without this, they have no mercy at all on a woman. Therefore, their claims of honoring women are a lie and false witness. Rather, such claims are, in all actuality, deceiving women and gradually drawing them into destruction."

Muhammad Taqi ul-Deen said, "And he (Pickthall) was truthful, because indeed I used to ride the train which goes underground in Berlin, and an elderly feeble woman would get on carrying two bags in her hands, and no one would stand for her. So, she would remain standing until some of the passengers got off. However, when they would see a young beautiful woman, they would rush to stand and offer their seats to her and she would know that they did not stand for her "for the sake of God" so she would

position of theirs does not coincide with their overall treatment of women. The truth is that excellence [and the truth of who is better] is in the hands of Allah, and it is not determined by masculinity or femininity; it is only determined by good deeds and wholesome character. Arabs have a saying: "Men are better than women, and a date is better than a locust". What they intend here is not that every man is better than every woman, nor that every date is better than every locust. The intent is preference of type, meaning men are [physically] stronger and more capable of doing labor than women. This is what is intended here with the preference [expressed]. Likewise, the general makeup of dates is better than the general makeup of locusts. And many women are better than a multitude of men, like Fatimah, Khadijah, Aishah, and before them, Aasiyah and Maryam. It is for this reason that al-Mutanabbi said, in his poem to Saif al-Daulah's sister,

و ما التأنيث لاسم الشمس عيب

---

therefore accept to sit in any of their seats unless she had an aim; so, sitting in the seat would be a sign of her acceptance of their flirting.

[TN] It suits here for me to mention the unfortunate fact that Marmaduke Pickthall (mentioned in the footnote above) - we pray that Allah grant him mercy - was heavily influenced by the misguided beliefs of the most prominent scholar of the deviant Mu'tazili creed, al-Zamakhshari. Though we do not seek to discredit any good done by Muslims, or non-Muslims for that matter, it is incumbent that we speak the truth, even if it is against ourselves, and that we highlight and correct each other's errors when it comes to the truth ~ for the betterment of us all and for the sake of Allah. Hence, the translation of the Quran done by Pickthall which is mentioned above is riddled with incorrect interpretations of various verses and concepts.

و لا التذكير فخر للهلال

و لو كان النساء كمن فقدنا

لفضلت النساء على الرجال

"The feminine case given to the word 'sun' [in
Arabic] is no point of shame [or weakness],
Nor is the masculine case given to the word
"crescent" a source of pride,
And if women [today] were like those [great]
women of old,
I would consider them better than men."

Furthermore, there are many locusts with abdomens full of
eggs, which are better than a hundred rotten dates, or than a
hundred of the worst kinds of dates which are like *hashfah*[9].
This is the viewpoint of those who eat locusts, and indeed the
Prophet (may the greatest blessings of Allah and peace be
upon him) ate them and he is an exemplary model for all who
eat them, while eating them is not mandatory.

After this introduction, I would like to begin with the specific
topic at hand with the help of the King, the Worshipped[10].
So, I hereby begin by saying ~ and all success is through Allah
~ al-Hafith ibn Katheer said when explaining the verse of
chapter al-Nisa that which, in brief, means: when the affair of
the two spouses worsens and discord is prolonged, the judge

---

[9] T.N.: A bad date which hardens and dries prematurely; it has no
sweetness nor is it fleshy, and it is seedless.
[10] T.N.: Translations of two names of Allah: the King الملك, and the
Worshipped المعبود.

18

appoints an upright referee from among the relatives of the woman and one from among the relatives of the man so that they can get together and collectively look into the affair of the couple in order to do that which would be best for the overall welfare of the couple. Based on their conclusions, they may decide that the couple separate, or they may conclude that they stay together. The Supreme Legislator (Allah) encourages that they stay together and for this reason, He says,

$$\text{إِن يُرِيدَآ إِصْلَـٰحًا يُوَفِّقِ ٱللَّهُ بَيْنَهُمَآ}$$

"As long as they truly seek to resolve the problem, Allah will guide them to success [in solving their issues]."

Moreover, Ali ibn Abu Talhah narrated from Ibn Abbass, "Allah, All-Mighty and Majestic, orders that they appoint a righteous man from the man's relatives and a similar man from the relatives of the woman. The two men must analyze the affairs to see which of the two spouses is at fault. If the man is at fault, they should separate him from his wife and restrict him to al-nafaqah[11]. Whereas if the woman is at fault, she should be ordered to stay with her husband yet be prevented from al-nafaqah. If their viewpoints (i.e. that of the two referees) coincide that they separate or remain together, it is lawful to implement their decision.

In addition, Ma'mar said, "Ibn Juraij informed us saying, 'Ibn Abu Maleekah told me that Aqeel ibn Abu Talib married

---

[11] T.N.: The mandatory financial support that the wife is entitled to

Fatimah bint Utbah ibn Abu Rabee'ah and that she said: "Be mine (i.e. marry me) and I'll spend on you financially". So, when he (Aqeel ibn Abu Talib) would go to her, she would say, "Where is Utbah ibn Rabee'ah and Shaybah ibn Rabee'ah?" He would reply, "Next to you, on your left side, in the Hellfire when you enter." So, she tore her garment (out of anger). She then went to Othman and told him what happened. He laughed and sent word to Ibn Abbass and Mu'awiyah. Ibn Abbass said, "I will indeed separate them," yet Mu'awiyah said, "I will not be the one to separate two people from among the people of Abdu Manaf." Thereafter, they found that the two had locked their doors; they had reconciled and returned to one another.

Abd ur-Razzaq reported, with his chain of narrators to Ubaydah, that he said, "I witnessed Ali when a woman once came to him with her husband, each of them with a group of people. So, one group put forward a referee and the other group put forward a referee as well. Thereby, Ali said to the two referees, "Do you two know what your responsibility is here? If you agree to keep them together, keep them together." The woman then said, "I accept [the ruling of] the Book of Allah, be it for me or against me." The husband said, "As for separation, no." Ali then said, "You have lied. You ultimately have no option but to accept [the ruling of] the Book of Allah - Most-High and Glorious - be it for you or against you." Then he said, "The scholars are in consensus that the two referees can join the two spouses or separate them." Even Ibrahim al-Nakhee said, "If the two referees decide to separate the two spouses with one pronouncement of divorce or two or three, they may do so"; and this is in a report from Malik. Further, Al-Hasan al-Basri said, "The two referees may judge with regards to keeping the spouses together but not to separate them." Qatadah and Zaid ibn Aslam said the same, and so did Ahmed ibn Hanbal, Abu Thor and Da'wud. Their reference for this is the statement of the Most-High (Allah),

$$إِن يُرِيدَآ إِصْلَٰحًا يُوَفِّقِ ٱللَّهُ بَيْنَهُمَآ$$

"As long as they truly seek to resolve the problem, Allah will guide them to success [in solving their issues]." [al-Nisa: 4:35]

Separation is not mentioned here. However, if they are two *wakeels* (legal representatives) from among the relatives of each of the two spouses, then their judgment is implemented whether it is to keep the spouses together or to separate them ~ and there is no difference of opinion concerning this.

Scholars of Islam have differed concerning the two referees and whether they must be designated by the ruler ~ whereby, they are authorized to rule even if the two spouses are not pleased [with their judgement] ~ or whether they are representatives appointed by the spouses. There are two viewpoints, yet most scholars hold the first viewpoint to be correct because of the statement of the Most-High,

$$﴿ فَٱبْعَثُوا۟ حَكَمًا مِّنْ أَهْلِهِۦ وَحَكَمًا مِّنْ أَهْلِهَآ ﴾$$

"... appoint a judge from his people and one from hers." [al-Nisa: 4:35]

Herein, He named them "referees" which entails judging affairs without necessarily pleasing those concerning whom judgement is being made; and this is the apparent meaning of the verse. This is also the latter position in the Shafi'ee school of thought, as it is also the position of Abu Haneefah and his companions. This is due to Ali's statement ~ may Allah have mercy on him ~ to that husband [mentioned above], "As for separation, then no," so, he said, "You have lied. Not until you comply as she has complied." Those who hold this position say, "If they were actually referees, a judge would need the compliance of the husband" ~ and Allah knows best.

Shaykh Abu Omar ibn Abd ul-Barr said, "There is a consensus of the scholars that if the two referees disagree, neither of their viewpoints are considered. There is also consensus among them that their viewpoints are indeed implemented with regards to keeping spouses together, even if they were not appointed by the husband and wife. Whereas scholars differed concerning whether their judgement for separation is to be implemented. Thereafter, Ibn Abd ul-Barr reported the consensus of scholars that their judgement be implemented in cases regarding separation as well, even if they have not been appointed by the spouses.

Here, let us present the statements of al-Qurtubi. Though there is some repetition for that which has preceded, we have still decided to present all of it because it is more suitable and complete [to present it comprehensively]. Also due to the fact that he referred to leading scholars who Moroccans are more familiar with than they are with others ~ even though the truth is not an affair of the east or the west ~ traversing the path authored [by a writer] to reach the truth is easier. It is authentically reported in a *hadith* that the Prophet (may the most special blessings of Allah and peace be upon him) said that he was never given a choice between to options except that he chose the easier of the two, as long as it did not involve breaking family ties, or something to that effect.

Al-Qurtubi said in his interpretation of the verse mentioned previously in His, the Most-High's, statement:

$$﴿ وَإِنْ خِفْتُمْ شِقَاقَ بَيْنِهِمَا ۞ ﴾$$

"And if you fear strife between them (the husband and wife)" [al-Nisa: 35]

The meaning of *shiqaq* (strife) preceded [this verse back] in chapter *al-Baqara*; it is as if each of the two spouses takes a piece of something (i.e. a viewpoint) opposing the piece (or viewpoint) of his (or her) spouse, meaning an angle other than that of his [or her] spouse. So, the meaning is "If you fear *shiqaqan*[12] (i.e. strife) between them, so it (the word *shiqaq*) was paired as *mudhaf* to the preposition[13]. This [style] is just like

---

23

when you say, "The movement of the moon-lit night pleases me," and likewise "The fasting of the day of Arafa." It states in the Revelation (al-Quran),

$$\{ بَلْ مَكْرُ ٱلَّيْلِ وَٱلنَّهَارِ ۝ \}$$

"Rather, it is the plotting of day and night." [al-Saba': 34:33]

It is also said that *baina* (the word in the verse which means "between") was used as a noun, and its state as a preposition was removed here because the meaning is "their situation" and "their marital relationship." So, it (the Qur'anic verse at hand) means: if you fear that their marital relationship and their companionship become distant "then appoint...". Concerning the verse "And if you fear...", contrary to that which has preceded, Sa'eed ibn Jubair said, "The ruling is that he (the husband) admonish her (his wife) first, so if she accepts [all is good] but if not, he should avoid her [in bed]; and if she

---

should have given examples in which the noun is paired with a preposition to better match [the phrase in the book] such as the phrase "Traversing the distance of a *farsakh* (an old length of measurement equal to the length of 3 miles approximately)". Moreover, when a noun is paired as the *mudhaf* with a preposition, the meaning is like that which is in His saying, highly exalted is He, "Nay, it is the plotting of day and night" which means planning by day and night; those who were arrogant would plot against the oppressed, aiming to land them in disbelief in Allah and worshipping rivals (false Gods) to Allah. See chapter Saba', verse 32.

Also, in His statement: "traveling of night" means traveling at night; "fasting of the Day of Arafa" means fasting on the Day of Arafa.

still does not conform, he should then hit her [lightly][14]. Thereafter, if she conforms [,all is good,] but if not, the judge must appoint a referee from his family and one from her family so that they can analyze who is causing the harm; and here is where the *khul'ah* occurs. However, it has been said that he has the right to hit [lightly) even before admonishing, though the prior position is more valid due to the order in the verse.

Secondly, the majority of scholars hold the understanding that the statement of Allah, "And if you fear..." is directed to the rulers and official leaders and that His statement, "As long as they truly seek to resolve the problem, Allah will guide them to success [in solving their issues]" is referring to the two referees; this is found in the position held by Ibn Abbass, Mujahid and others and it means that if the two referees truly seek to resolve the problem, then Allah will guide the spouses to success [in solving their issues]. Yet, it is also said that the meaning is [if] the two spouses [truly intend to resolve the problem]. This means that if the spouses truly want to resolve the affair and are truthful in what they explain to the two referees concerning the matter, "Allah will guide them to success [in solving their issues]". It is also said that this is directed to the responsible guardians. He says, "if your fear" meaning if you know of trouble between two spouses then "appoint a referee from the man's family and a referee from

---

[14] T.N.: The "hit" here is a light one, not a hit that hurts or harms the wife, but, again, a light hit intended to bring the wife's attention to the severity of her transgression when she has taken her obstinance too far.

the woman's family." This is because such guardians [selected from among the spouses' family] are more familiar with the circumstances of the husband and wife.

Furthermore, the two [referees] should be of upright character, sound perspective, insight and *fiqh* (understanding of religion). In a case in which there are no such individuals from the families of the spouses, they should appoint two individuals who are not from the family yet are of upright character and are knowledgeable and this is [only] when their issue has become very problematic, and they do not know which one of them is the source of the mistreatment. Whereas, if the guilty one [of the spouses] is known, then the rights of the [wronged] spouse must be regained [and upheld], and the one causing harm is forced to desist from causing harm.

Furthermore, it is said that the referee from the relatives of the husband should meet the husband in privacy and say, "Tell me what you feel inside; do you desire to be with her or not? So that I can know what you really want." If he says, "I have no need for her. Get whatever you can from her for me and separate us," it would then be known that the discord stems from him. Whereas, if he says, "I want to be with her, so give her of my wealth whatever you will to please her and do not separate us," it would then be known that he is not the source of the discord.

In addition, the referee from the family of the wife should meet with her (and ask), "Do you desire to be with your husband or not?"[15] If she says, "Separate us, and give whatever you will of my wealth," it would then be known that the

---

[15] Muhammd Taqi al-Deen, the author of this book said: His saying "Do you desire (pronounced in Arabic *tahween*) ..." with a *kasra* on the "*wow*" (و) and it becomes *yahwa* with a *fatha*. It means: do you love your husband? This is proof that it is not permissible to force a woman to remain with someone she does not desire and become like some animal of utility; as if she has no value and is merely a tool to be utilized in the hand of the husband with which he can do whatever he wants. Ignorant judges do not reflect upon this, the actual meaning, so they issue haphazard, destructive rulings severely oppressing the wife and demeaning her by forcing her to remain with a man she does not love. Some of the judges of Morocco have said to me that the Moroccan legal system looks into the affairs of the husband and wife; if they have children, they are obligated to remain together, despite their true feelings. Whereas if they do not have children, it does not obligate either of them [to remain with the other]. If one of them rebels, they are imprisoned until he or she conforms. And if we only knew, when a woman refuses to remain with her husband and says, "I do not love him nor do I trust him," and we rule that she be imprisoned, do we take her and her children? In addition, concerning the police officer who takes her, an *anjabi* (non-related man having no right to be alone with her), do they all stay in the prison and remain there days and nights until the woman complies to this oppressive law. Extend to her and her children a thousand greetings of peace! How can she take care of the affairs of her children, and what would happen to her honor and reputation? Whether she submits to her husband, who is in opposition to her, or whether he divorces her, and she desires to marry another man this law causes damage to a woman's reputation, damage to her children, and there is absolutely no benefit. If she conforms and returns [to her husband] today, despite her true feelings, she is like a slave who flees but is returned to slavery because, in reality, she will only remain with him until she finds the chance to flee, leaving the children to be lost [and neglected]. She may even commit suicide. However, the *Shari'ah* of the best of all of mankind [Prophet Muhammad] is free from such a law.

Those who issue such verdicts may say, "We have only issued this ruling out of our great concern for something which is called "protection of the family" with those who do not know Arabic, out of fear that the children will be lost [and neglected]. I say in response that Islam is more merciful with children and parents than you! Therefore, it has established the law

discord stems from her. However, if she says, "Do not separate us but encourage him to increase the amount he gives me for my financial needs, and to be good to me," it would then be known that she is not the source of the discord.

When the source of the discord has become clear to the two referees, they must then approach that particular spouse with admonishment, firm condemnation and mandate that he or she desists. And this is in His, the Most-High's, statement,

---

of the khul'ah so that she who is in a hole can get out of that hole [and be done with it]. If the woman is able to take care of her children financially, the mandatory financial responsibility is no longer his responsibility, and the woman must return the dowry she received, and what more should he expect from her? On the other hand, if she is unable to take care of the children financially, and she insists on divorce, it is fine for them to divorce and cooperate with each other, sharing financial responsibility of the children. However, if the mother is unable, it is mandatory for the father to handle things himself. Furthermore, if the woman is unable to return the dowry or even some of it, she is excused from having to give it back:

$$لا يكلف الله نفسا الا وسعها$$

Meaning, "Allah does not burden anyone with more that he can bear." [al-Baqarah: 286].

Also, it is not just nor is it of true manhood that we say to him, "Take her by the ear and sell her in the slave market with her children for financial gain; marry someone else, and leave her with her children in "the valley of the lost."

Concerning his statement, "They (i.e. cases of disobedience or disobedient women) either return to obedience," means that if nushuz (marital discord) occurs between spouses then they reestablish obedience, which means that they reconcile and their relationship is once again healthy and good, and they treat each other with love again; [they say that] there is then no need for the two referees. This is what he meant when he said, "If the prior occurs, they (the two spouses) are left alone."

$$\{ \text{فَٱبْعَثُوا۟ حَكَمًا مِّنْ أَهْلِهِۦ وَحَكَمًا مِّنْ أَهْلِهَآ} ۞ \}$$

"And if you fear strife between them (the husband and wife)" [al-Nisa: 4: 35]

Thirdly, the scholars say that this verse has categorized women logically since women are either obedient or disobedient, and cases of disobedience either return to obedience or they do not. If the prior occurs (meaning if the woman returns to obedience), they (the two spouses) are left alone. This is based on the narration reported by al-Nasa'i that Aqeel ibn AbuTalib married Fatimah bint Utbah ibn Rabee'ah[16]. So,

---

[16] Fatimah bint Utbah is from Bani Umayyah and her husband, Aqeel ibn Abu Talib, is from Bani Hashim.

Her father was Utbah ibn Rabee'ah, and her paternal uncle was Shaibah ibn Rabee'ah, and they were both killed in the battle of Badr while both were still disbelievers. As for Utbah, it is mentioned in the book on history of Ibn Hashim that Ishaq and "Utbah bin Rabee'ah ibn Abd Shams said that Ubaidah ibn al-Harith ibn Abd al-Muttalib killed him." However, Ibn Hisham said, "He shared in killing him along with Hamza and Ali."

According to Shaibah, Ibn Ishaq said, "Hamza ibn Abd al-Muttalib killed Shaibah ibn Rabee'ah ibn Abd Shams."

So, one of those who shared in killing her father was the brother of her husband, and that was Ali ibn Abu Talib, and Hamza was her husband's uncle. All three of them were from Bani Hashim. In addition, her uncle was the one who killed Hamza ibn Abd al-Muttalib, the paternal uncle of the Prophet (may the most special blessings of Allah be upon him and peace) and paternal uncle of her husband, Aqeel, as well.

This is the reason for which she said to her husband, "By Allah, my heart does not love you, Oh Bani Hashim!" So, this was the tribalist bias of *jahiliyah* (i.e., the days of ignorance before the commission of Prophet Muhammad, Allah's special blessings and peace be upon him) in her which one would fear might become a blemish on her faith as a result. This is because she would thereby hate Bani Hashim because they killed her father and her uncle in a war the leader of which was the Messenger of Allah

whenever he would go to her, she would say, "Oh, Children of Hashim! Wallahi my heart will never love you! Where are

---

(may the most special blessings of Allah be upon him and peace), a war in which Allah aided His *awliya* (His allies from among mankind, the most beloved of His creation to Him) and defeated His enemies. Therefore, it is incumbent that every believer takes the *awliya* of Allah as *awilyaa*, even if they annihilated one's extended family, and that every believer takes the enemies of Allah as enemies even if they were one's closest family member. Allah, the Most-High, says in Chapter *al-Tawbah*,

يا أيها الذين آمنوا لا تتخذوا آباءكم و إخوانكم أولياء ان استحبوا الكفر على الايمان و من يتولهم منكم فأولئك هم الظالمين

[which means "Oh you who believe, do not take your fathers and brothers as allies if they choose disbelief over faith. Furthermore, whoever does take them as allies then they truly are wrongdoers." [al-Tawbah: verse 23] Additionally, in her statement "Where are those whose necks are like silver vessels?" Here, she was describing her father, her uncle and those who were killed of her extended family, as having long necks, which is a much-desired attribute of beauty [and physical attractiveness]. Arabs consider this a sign of honorable lineage; this is their claim. Also, in her statement, "Their noses draw towards their mouths" means that they have a nose structure in which the bone is slightly raised. In Lisan al-Arab, the author says, "Al-shumam is when the bone of the nose is raised while the uppermost part is even with the tip of the nose slightly elongated. If the nose bears curvage, this is called al-qana. Therefore, [for example] it is said that a man is ashamm al-anf (i.e., one with an elegantly raised nose). Furthermore, Arabs assert that a raised nose is proof of a noble origin. K'ab ibn Zuhair said in his poem "Banat Su'ad", which should really be called "The Poem of the burdah (a shawl-like garment or covering)" because the Prophet (may the most special blessing of Allah be upon him and peace) covered him with a burdah when he recited it in front of him and he pardoned him:

شم العرانين أبطال, لبوسهم   من نسخ داود, في الهيجا, سرابيل

The mighty forefathers are brave men, their garments like that of Dawud (David), in harsh war, armor.

those whose necks are like the vessels of silver? Their noses draw towards their mouths. Where is Utbah ibn Rabee'ah?" Aqeel would remain silent. Until one day, he went to her, and he was depressed. She said, "Where is Utbah ibn Rabee'ah?" So, he replied, "He'll be to your left side in the Hellfire when you enter." So, she pulled her garment over her and went to Othman. She told him what happened. He then sent Ibn Abbas and Mu'awiyah. Ibn Abbas said, "Indeed I will separate them." Mu'awiyah said, "I will not separate two leaders from the Children of Abu Manaf." Thereafter, they went to them and found that they had locked their door and solved their issues.

If they had, however, found that the two were [still] in opposition and had not reconciled, and their issues had become exacerbated, they (Abbass and Mu'awiyah) would have worked hard to bring about the desired connection between them, and they would have reminded them of Allah and of [the importance of] their relationship. Thereafter, if they were to reconcile and return to one another, Abbass and Mu'awiyah would stay out of their affair [as they did]. Though, if they had done other than that and took the stance that they must separate, they would have divorced them. They would have had the right to divorce the husband and wife [in this case]. This would be done regardless of what a local judge rules, or if he opposes them, and whether the husband and wife appointed them as *wakeelan* (i.e., two official appointed representatives) or not. Further, their separation of the spouses [in this case] is a permanent divorce.

Others have said that referees are not permitted to divorce spouses if the husband has not authorized them and official representatives [in the matter], and they must inform the *imam* (leader, person of authority in the area). This is based on the fact that they are [in essence] two messengers and witnesses. It is then that the *imam* may separate [the spouses] if he wants and order the referee to separate the two spouses. This is one of the positions of al-Shafi', and al-Kufiyun also held this position. It is also the position of Ataa ibn Zaid and al-Hasan, and Abu Thor. However, the correct position is the first, which is that the two referees are permitted to divorce spouses even when they have not been authorized [by the two spouses]. This is the position of Malik, al-Awza'i and Ishaq. It has also been reported to have been the position held by Othman, Ali, Ibn Abbas, al-Sha'bee, al-Nakh'ee, and it is was also held by al-Shafi'ee. This is because Allah, the Most-High, says,

﴿ فَٱبۡعَثُواْ حَكَمٗا مِّنۡ أَهۡلِهِۦ وَحَكَمٗا مِّنۡ أَهۡلِهَآ ٣٥ ﴾

"And if you fear strife between them (the husband and wife), appoint a judge from his people and one from hers." [al-Nisa: 4: 35]

This is text directly from Allah, highly exalted above all imperfections, clarifying that the two [referees] are judges, not representatives, nor witnesses. A representative has a particular name (*wakeel*) in the *Shari'ah*, and a particular meaning. Likewise, the referee has a particular name (*hakam*) in the *Shari'ah*, and a particular meaning. Therefore, since Allah has made clear what each of them are, no one ~ especially a scholar ~ should apply the meaning of one of them to the other.

Al-Daraqutni reported in a *hadith* of Muhammad ibn Sireen concerning this verse,

﴿ وَإِنۡ خِفۡتُمۡ شِقَاقَ بَيۡنِهِمَا فَٱبۡعَثُوا۟ حَكَمٗا مِّنۡ أَهۡلِهِۦ وَحَكَمٗا مِّنۡ أَهۡلِهَآ ۚ ۞ ﴾

"And if you fear strife between them (the husband and wife), appoint a judge from his people and one from hers. [al-Nisa: 4:35]

Ubaydah said, "A man and woman came to Ali, each one of them with a group of people. So, one group put forward a referee and the other group put forward a referee as well. Thereby, Ali said to the two referees, "Do you two know what you must do? If you agree to separate them, then separate them." The woman then said, "I accept [the ruling of] the Book of Allah, be it for me or against me." The husband said, "As for separation, no." Ali then said, "You have lied. You ultimately have no option but to take the position that she has taken." This narration has an authentic chain of narrators. It has also been reported from Ali, by way of various reliable sources, from Ibn Sireen from Ubaydah. This is what Abu Omar said. Notice here that if they were representatives or witnesses, he would not have said "Do you two know what your responsibility is here?" This point is clear.

Abu Haneefah used the statement of Ali, may Allah be pleased with him, to the husband as evidence when he said, "You ultimately have no option but to accept [the terms] just as she has accepted [them]." This points the fact that per his *mathab* (school of Islamic jurisprudence), the spouses must not be separated without the agreement of the husband, and that the foundational rule, which scholars have consensus on, is that divorce is in the hands of the husband and in the hand of whomever he entrusts with that authority. Whereas, Malik and those who follow him hold that it is considered divorce by way of the *sultan* (official leader and authority) for *al-mulee* and for *al-"aneen* (the impotent).[17]

---

[17] *Al-mulee* is a noun which names one who does the act of *alaa* (past tense), *yulee* (present tense), and *elaa* (a form similar to the gerund in English grammar). Allah, the Most-High, said in chapter al-Baqarah, verses 226

$$\text{لِّلَّذِينَ يُؤْلُونَ مِن نِّسَائِهِمْ تَرَبُّصُ أَرْبَعَةِ أَشْهُرٍ ۖ فَإِن فَاءُوا فَإِنَّ اللَّهَ غَفُورٌ رَّحِيمٌ}$$

$$\text{وَإِنْ عَزَمُوا الطَّلَاقَ فَإِنَّ اللَّهَ سَمِيعٌ عَلِيمٌ}$$

meaning "those who take oaths not to have sexual intercourse with their wives (*al-ilaa*) must abstain from having sex with them for four months; if they reconcile thereafter, indeed Allah is Oft-Forgiving, Most-Merciful; and if they insist to divorce, then Allah is All-Hearing and All-Wise."

Al-Ilaa is for a man to make an oath that he will not have sex with his wife for a period of time, whether that period be four months or less, it's permissible. More than four months is not permissible. As for the woman, she can request after the four month period that he either have sex with her or divorce her. If he refuses, the ruler (authorities) can divorce them. It is reported that Aishah said that the Prophet (may Allah's most special blessings be upon him and peace) took an oath (*ilaa*) from his women for a month ~ al-Bukhari and Muslim reported this narration.

Concerning the term he used, *al-a'neen*, the author of *Lisan* said, "*al-a'neen* is a man that does not have sex with women, nor does he desire them."

Muhammad Taqi al-Deen says, "And there is an issue with his statement '... nor does he desire them,' because if he does not desire them, why marry? Further, why would he refuse to divorce [his wife] causing the ruler (authorities) to divorce them. Conversely, it seems [more plausible] that it is *al-a'neen*, with a *kasrah* on the *ain* and the *nun* with *shaddah*; it is similar to the word structure of the word *skeet*. Such a man is the one who cannot have sex. This meaning is the meaning that [the book] al-*Lisan* in essence means. If one says, "Why has the language of today differed [from that of old] stating that it is specifically to do with sex? It does not express that

34

Fourthly, in a case in which the two referees differ, their judgements are not implemented. None of their views must be carried out except those they agree upon. Such is the case with every two referees who judge on an issue. So, if one of them held that the husband and wife should be separated and the other did not, or if one of them held that there should be a financial payment made and the other did not, none of this matters unless they agree. Malik said concerning referees implementing the three divorces, "One divorce is implemented, and they cannot separate spouses divorcing them with more than one permanent divorce." Further, the

---

this is the act of having sex." The answer is that this phrase is null and void, [a product of] colonialism, and has nothing to do with the Arabic language. This is because sex itself is a *kinayah* (metaphor). Arabs would use various metaphors to express this act such as *al-jima'* as well as *al-mubasharah*. For example, the Most-High says, " وَلَا تُبَاشِرُوهُنَّ وَأَنتُمْ عَاكِفُونَ فِي الْمَسَاجِد" meaning "and do not have sexual intercourse with them while you are adhering to seclusion in a mosque" [al-Qur'an, Chapter al-Baqarah: 187]. As for the term *al-mass*, an example is in the statement of the Most-High,

وَإِن طَلَّقْتُمُوهُنَّ مِن قَبْلِ أَن تَمَسُّوهُنَّ وَقَدْ فَرَضْتُمْ لَهُنَّ فَرِيضَةً فَنِصْفُ مَا فَرَضْتُمْ

meaning "If you divorce your wives before consummating, and you have given them a dowry, you may retrieve half of what you gave them." [al-Qur'an, Chapter al-Baqarah: 237]. As for *al-ityan* (entering one's wife), it is like that which is mentioned in the *hadith*, "Indeed, he who enters his wife in her buttocks has indeed committed an act of disbelief," and Arabs are not poor when it comes to words [and language]. No doubt, their language is the richest of all languages. Nor are they [poor] in literature; they (the Arabs) preceded the colonizers to it (i.e., the arts of language and literature) by a multitude of centuries. This is an example of erasing language and humiliating [oneself and culture] for colonizers ~ we ask that Allah pardon us [and keep us away from such actions].

35

position of Ibn al-Qasim[18] is [in his statement], "The three divorces must be implemented if they agree upon it." Al-Mughirah held this position, as well as Ashab, Ibn al-Majishoon and Asbag. Ibn al-Mawaz said, "If one of them holds that one divorce must be implemented and the other holds that three must be implemented, only one is implemented. However, Ibn Habeeb said that Asbag said that it (counting it as three divorces) is not even considered.

Fifthly, sending one [referee] is sufficient because Allah (highly exalted above all imperfections) ruled that there [must be] four witnesses in affairs of fornication. The Prophet (may the most special blessings of Allah be upon him and peace) sent Anees alone[19] to a woman who had committed fornication. The Prophet said to him, "If she confesses, stone her." Abd al-Malik said the same in "Al-Mudawanah". Therefore, I assert that if sending only one is lawful, it would be sufficient for a husband and wife to appoint only one referee, and holding it as permissible is the most suitable position as long as the spouses agree. Moreover, if a husband and wife appoint two referees, and they issue their judgement, their judgment is carried out. This is because our position is that the

---

[18] Concerning Ibn al-Qasim's statement, "The three divorces must be implemented if they agree upon this." This statement is contradictory, so it must be analyzed. Regarding this, Malik said, "They cannot divorce spouses except as one permanent divorce, meaning three divorces are not required, even if they agree upon that. So, requiring three [divorces] opposes the position of Malik; therefore, it is incorrect to build the statement of Ibn al-Qasim and those after him upon the position of Malik.

[19] *Hadith* Anees and the woman is found in al-Bukhari.

appointment of referees to judge is lawful. And thereby, the judgement made must be implemented in all relevant affairs.

This is the case when each of the two are *'adl* (upright in character and their practice of the religion); whereas, if they are not *'adl*, Malik said, "The judgement is rendered null because the two referees present an unnecessary risk." Ibn al-Arabi said, "The correct position is to implement their judgment, because in a case in which they are appointed as representatives (*wakeelan*), whatever an appointed representative decides must be applied. Further, if they are appointed as referees, the husband and wife have given them precedence over themselves [to represent them] and the danger [which lies in the referee not being *adl*] does not impact [their status as having been appointed as referees] just as it does not impact in the case of them being appointed as representatives. Moreover, the field of law, as a whole, involves [an aspect of] risk and danger, and it is not necessary that one being judged have knowledge of what a final judgement will look like [in any particular case]. Ibn al-Arabi said, "Allah addressed the affair of the two referees and has legislated this [practice] in cases in which [serious] marital discord and [major] differences between spouses occur. This is an extremely important affair about which the Muslim nation, as a whole, has agreed concerning its foundations in the religion, though they may differ concerning particular details related to this practice. However, strangely,[20] the people of our country are not aware of what the *Book* and the *Sunnah* mandate concerning these affairs. They say, "their affair (that of the spouses with marital trouble] is to be put in the hands of a trustworthy individual", and this is in complete opposition to the text [of the Qur'an and *Sunnah*] as is clear to

---

indeed sought support from other experts [in clarifying the correct approach] in these affairs yet no one came to my aid except for one judge", he is expressing that he called on the judges of Morocco in his era to implement the *Book* of Allah and the *Sunnah* of His messenger, as well as the consensus of the Muslim nation, and of them Malik and the scholars with him. They were arrogant and stubbornly opposed, except for one judge who answered his call for support. With this being the case in those times, and nearly nine hundred years have passed, what then can we expect to be the state of affairs these days, which are the worst of times? Nevertheless, we praise Allah, because there are still those in Morocco who call people to the implementation of this *Sunnah*.

In his statement, "So, when Allah granted me authority over these issues, I enacted the *Sunnah* [in these affairs] as should be the case." Ibn al-Arabi was never the king of Morocco, but he was the *amir* of Ceuta and surrounding areas during a period of turmoil that occurred at his time. So, the Leader of the Believers, his highness, al-Hasan II, is the most suitable individual to revive this *Sunnah* practice. A *Sunnah* which is the *Sunnah* of his grandfather (i.e., his forefather), al-Mustafa (may the most special blessings of Allah and peace be upon him), and which is found in the *Book* of Allah (highly exalted above all imperfections); in addition to its being the consensus of the Muslim nation. Allah has indeed made him king and blessed him with support and strength which none of the kings of the time of Ibn al-Arabi had, so how much more can he do? In reviving the *Sunnah* practice of appointing the two referees, there is undeniable elevation of the status of the Moroccan woman, an abolishment of oppression against women, and protection of their honor. We ask that Allah bless him with success in achieving this and reviving many other *Sunnah* practices, as well as doing away with *bid'ah* (innovation in religion). May Allah bless him in his age by giving him a long life so that he can achieve the reformation that he seeks to achieve, the reformation that all good Moroccan people want ~ indeed Allah is All-Hearing, He who answers those who call on Him.

see. They have neither complied with the *Book of Allah* nor have they applied any sound analysis, and this is undoubtedly in clear opposition to the Qur'an and *Sunnah*. I indeed sought support from other experts [in clarifying the correct approach] in these affairs, yet no one came to my aid except for one judge; nor did I find the support of any other expert in the affair of issuing a ruling based on an individual's swearing by Allah ~ in addition to there also being a witness ~ except the support of one other judge. So, when Allah granted me authority over these issues, I enacted the *Sunnah* [in these affairs] as should be the case. So, do not find it strange that the people of our country are blinded by ignorance. However, be shocked concerning Abu Haneefah; he holds that the two referees are not informed enough to judge in the affairs of spouses. Rather, be double-shocked concerning al-Shafi'ee because he said, "That which resembles the apparent meaning of the verse is that it addresses both husband and wife, treating them similarly in these affairs." He said, "This is because I saw that Allah, Mighty and Glorious, allows quarrelling spouses to reconcile and repair their relationship. Likewise, he allows the *khul'ah* when they fear they will not uphold the rights which Allah has ordained [for each spouse], and this is practically based on the preference of the woman. He also forbids that the husband takes back anything which he has given [his wife] when he decides to divorce her in order to marry someone else. So, when he legislated that we appoint two referees when we fear serious marital discord, this is evidence that the judgement of the two referees is independent of the spouses' judgement [concerning their problems]. That being the case, they should appoint a referee from his relatives and a referee

39

from her relatives, and none other than two trustworthy individuals should be responsible for [selecting and] appointing the two referees ~ with the consent and full trust of the husband and wife ~ whether the referees choose to reunite them or separate them, if they so see fit. Ultimately, this proves that the referees are *wakeelan* (authorized representatives) of the husband and wife."

Ibn al-Arabi said, "This is the gist of al-Shafi'i's argument, and his fellow scholars [who agree with his positions in general] celebrate this position of his; even though, it does not deserve to be considered plausible, nor is it becoming of someone of such a high caliber of knowledge. Judge Abu Ishaq, took it upon himself to refute al-Shafi', though most of his rebuttal did not do justice. As for al-Shafi''s statement, 'That which resembles the apparent meaning of the verse is that it addresses both husband and wife'; this is incorrect. Rather, that is exactly what the text addresses [not merely appearing that way], and it is from among the clearest and most unambiguous verses in the Qur'an. Indeed, Allah, the Most-High says,

$$ ﴿ ٱلرِّجَالُ قَوَّٰمُونَ عَلَى ٱلنِّسَآءِ ۞ ﴾ $$

"Men are responsible and in authority over women."
[al-Nisa: 4:34]

So, whoever fears *nushuz* (marital discord) instigated by his wife, he should advise her with words of guidance, and if she [desists and] draws near then all is good. However, if she does

40

not desist, he should refrain from sexual relations with her. If she discontinues causing problems, all is good. However, if she persists, he should then hit her [lightly, in a manner which does not harm but draws attention to the seriousness of the problem]. If she continues her excessive behavior, this is when the two referees visit them. If this is not clear text, then there is nothing clear in the Qur'an! Further, let us say it is not exactly as the text clearly states it; let us say it is "that which is apparent". So then, how does al-Shafi' say, 'That which resembles the apparent meaning...'. We have no idea what 'resembled the apparent meaning' means. Then he said, "He allows the *khul'ah'* when they fear they will not uphold the rights which Allah has ordained [for each spouse], and this is practically based on the preference of the woman." On the contrary, the *khul'ah'* absolutely must be based on the preference of the woman. This is exactly what the text states. Then he said, "So, when he legislated that we appoint two referees when we fear serious marital discord, this is evidence that the judgement of the two referees is independent of the spouses' judgement [concerning their problems]."

Therefore, the one who appoints the referee must be other than them (the husband and wife), so that whatever the final judgement is, it can be implemented regardless of the preference of the husband and wife. This way, the obligation that the affair be resolved by a third party is fulfilled. As for a case in which the referees judge based on that which the spouses ordered them as representatives, they would not have then made independent, unbiased judgement; hence, the obligation that a third party resolve the issue would not be fulfilled. As for his statement, 'With the permission and authorization of the husband and wife', this is an outright mistake, because Allah (highly exalted above all imperfections) indeed addressed [a third party] other than the husband and wife when there is a fear of serious marital discord between spouses. He ordered that two referees be sent and since other than the husband and wife are addressed in this instance, how then would their authorization be needed? Furthermore, their judgement is not valid unless they both agree upon that position. This is a balanced refutation of al-Shafi' based on thorough research of the related evidence. Contrary to the statement of the *khawarij* that, 'Judgement is for no one other than Allah, the Most-High.' Truthful words with which they intend to support their erroneous beliefs and positions." The quote [of Ibn al-Arabi] ends here.

An Explanation of Concepts Which Readers May Find Difficult to Grasp

There are various related issues here:

First: His statement "... and you all fear" is different from that which is in the previous verse. This is concerning the statement of the Most-High,

﴿ وَٱلَّٰتِی تَخَافُونَ نُشُوزَهُنَّ ۝ ﴾

"And concerning wives who you fear will cause
serious marital discord" [al-Nisa: 4:34]

Al-Qurtubi said, Ibn Abbass said, 'You must know and be certain' and it is said that it should be 'at his door.'" His statement "at his door" means that fear [of marital discord] is at his door. It is not referring to knowledge or certainty. The correct position is that of Ibn Abbas because a man should not pass judgement on whether his wife has caused discord, or not, merely based on assumptions or a biased understanding. The manifestations of serious marital discord (nushuz) must be clear. Further, nushuz is transgression, taken from the word al-nashz which means rising up. It is as if to say one of the spouses has become extremely arrogant considering him or herself above their spouse, holding him or herself higher than their rightful position, thereby causing great harm in the marriage. The statement of the Most-High in chapter al-Mujadalah addresses when Allah says,

$$\{ \text{وَإِذَا قِيلَ ٱنشُزُوا فَٱنشُزُوا} \circledast \}$$

"And when it is said, 'Get up and go', get up and go."

[al-Mujadalah: 11]

Moreover, *nushuz* can be from a man or a woman just as the Most-High says in this very chapter, verse 128,

$$\{ \text{وَإِنِ ٱمْرَأَةٌ خَافَتْ مِنۢ بَعْلِهَا نُشُوزًا أَوْ إِعْرَاضًا فَلَا جُنَاحَ عَلَيْهِمَآ أَن يُصْلِحَا بَيْنَهُمَا صُلْحًا وَٱلصُّلْحُ} \circledast \}$$

"So, if a woman fears *nushuz* from her husband or that he will ignore and neglect her, there is no blame upon them if they come to an amicable agreement with one another that can solve their problems; such agreements which rectify affairs are good."

Al-Qurtubi said [in explanation of this verse], "*Al-nushuz* is when he distances himself from her. While *al-i'raad*[21] is when he does not speak with her or enjoy her company.

Second:

Scholars say that when a man sees the manifestations of serious marital discord in his wife, the first thing he should begin with in order to rectify their condition is to advise her with words of guidance and remind her of Allah, of His verses, and of the *Hadeeth* of His Messenger (may the most special

---

[21] T.N.: *Al-i'raad* refers to the original term in the verse (إعراض) which I have translated as "ignore and neglect". The Arabic word literally means to turn away from someone or something.

44

blessings of Allah be upon him and peace). If he does not find success with that, he should then avoid her – and scholars differed concerning this avoidance (al-hajr). Is it that he refrain from having sexual intercourse with her, turning his back to her [in bed], or does he refrain from sleeping in the same bed with her and from talking to her?

Third:

If the steps which have preceded do not have the desired impact on her, he should then hit her [lightly], a hit which is not painful. Al-Qurtubi said, "And the hitting mentioned in this verse is for the purpose of establishing good character and practices, not hard hitting which hurts. Such hitting does not break bones, nor does it leave bruising or injury as does punching and the likes. This is because the only intended result is rectifying the issues at hand. Therefore, without doubt, if hitting leads to death, the culprit must be recompensed in the same manner. Muhammad Taqi al-Deen said, "Al-lakz is punching someone anywhere on the body; however, it is also said that it is only in the chest. Balling up the fist [or punching] is what Moroccans call al-dabzah. Whereas, in the language of the colonialists it is called al-buniyah. Al-Qurtubi said, "Ataa said, 'I said to Ibn Abbass, 'What is this type of hitting which isn't hard and does not hurt?' He said, 'With siwak [22] and the likes'" – end of quote.

---

[22] T.N.: Siwak is a small pencil-like stick used traditionally by Muslims for cleaning one's teeth. It is usually around the size of a pencil or pen in both length and width.

Muhammad Taqi al-Deen said, "The time has come for us ~ oh assembly of Muslim authors and thinkers ~ that we research the affair of hitting so that we build [our teachings, positions, arguments] on a firm foundation. This is because the enemies of Islam from among the Europeans and Americans[23] and those who claim Islam yet follow them, those who portray an image that they have great respect for women and outright declare their worship of them; they do this to deceive women, that they lower their guard and disgrace themselves, in turn leading them to their own destruction. They cannot imagine a man hitting his woman in any way whatsoever.

---

[23] I was in Bonn, Germany living in the home of an elderly woman. She had two rooms for rent. One was my room and the other was for a German student. This student had a girlfriend whom he called his fiancé. She would come to him in the early afternoon on Saturday and stay with him until Sunday morning as is their common practice. One day, he brought two English students, young ladies, and the elderly woman got extremely angry. She said in German, "Ieh have kein harim hier" which means "I am not running a harem here!" A harem, from their viewpoint, is the home of a Muslim in which he gathers numerous wives and traps them there in order to take pleasure in them sexually and has them serve him, not allowing them to leave or see anyone. Moreover, they claim that this is the ugliest thing that Islam has introduced to the world. So, once she calmed down, I clarified to her that she had a grave misunderstanding. I explained that this harem which Muslims are accused of has no true existence except for in tales which are attributed to caliphs and kings of the past. Further, when she said "I am not running a harem here" she was, in essence, saying that it is not permitted for any other girl to enter her home other than his known girlfriend whom he calls his fiancé. That is custOmary for them and there is no shame in that according to them. However, for him to bring different girls as he pleases, she considers that degradation of her home, or as if her home were a whorehouse. At that point, I wrote an article entitled, "I Am Not Running a Harem" and I sent it to Fath Magazine, owned by Muhib al-Deen al-Khateeb (may Allah have mercy on him). It was published there in 1937 on the Christian calendar.

They disparage Islam and hold that the *Shari'ah* allowing hitting is shameful. I will exert all efforts, seeking the help of Allah, to address this issue with words which will defend against enemies of Islam and refute those Muslims of horrible understandings, and hard, heavy hearts; those Muslims who have gone to extremes concerning the permissibility of hitting, including the limits of this practice, the means and type of hitting, as well as the reasons for which it becomes permissible.

The details of these affairs are encapsulated in four categories:

1. The reason for hitting
2. The type of hitting
3. The purpose
4. The legal ruling in the *Shari'ah*

As for the reason (number 1), some of its explanation has preceded above. It involves her disobedience and refusing to obey her husband with regards to sexual intercourse and the related intimate sexual relations which precede sex, her ignoring her husband and callous behavior towards him. Furthermore, since the Qur'an is interpreted using the sayings and actions of the Prophet (may the most special blessings of Allah and peace be upon him), it is incumbent that we interpret this issue with the sayings and actions of the Prophet (may the most special blessings of Allah and peace be upon him). Surely, he is the most knowledgeable concerning the revelation that Allah has sent down. Indeed, Allah says in chapter al-Nahl, verse 44,

47

$$\{ \text{وَأَنزَلْنَآ إِلَيْكَ ٱلذِّكْرَ لِتُبَيِّنَ لِلنَّاسِ مَا نُزِّلَ إِلَيْهِمْ وَلَعَلَّهُمْ يَتَفَكَّرُونَ} ﴿٤٤﴾ \}$$

"And We have sent the revelation down to you so that you can make clear for all people that which has been sent down to them, that they might ponder [its message and meanings]."

Al-Qurtubi said, "And in *Saheeh Muslim*, '**Be mindful of and dutiful to Allah (i.e. have *taqwa*) in your treatment of women, because, indeed, you have married them as a trust from Allah. You have sought permission to be with them sexually by the word of Allah. Further, you have the right that they do not allow anyone that you do not like into your home. If they do, hit them lightly, a hit which is not painful.'**[24] ... to the end of the *hadith*. He reported it from the long *hadith* of Jabir during *hajj*. It means that wives should not allow anyone from among relatives or non-relative women whom you do not like into your home. The report from al-Tirmithi of 'Amr ibn al-Ahwas, which al-Tirmithi authenticated, is based on this, in which he ('Amr) observed *hajj* with the Messenger of Allah (may the most special blessings of Allah and peace be upon him). He (the Prophet) praised Allah and extolled Him; He reminded and advised [those there] saying, **"You must be good to women because surely they are young ladies for whom you are responsible; you do not have any right [concerning the matter] other than that, unless they commit a commit a clear act of**

---

[24] Muslim (*hadith* 1218)

disloyalty or treachery. Then, if they were to do that, do not have sex with them, and hit them lightly, a hit which is not painful. Yet, if they obey you, do not seek to make anything difficult for them. Surely, you have a right over your women, and your women have a right over you. As for your right over your women: they must not allow anyone you do not like to sit in your home, nor should they [even] allow anyone you do not like into your home. Moreover, their (women's) right over you is that you treat them very well by providing good clothes and food for them."[25] Al-Tirmithi graded this a *hadith hasan saheeh*. In the Prophet's statement "commit a clear act of disloyalty or treachery", he means that they must not allow anyone whom their husbands hate [into their homes] or cause their husbands to become angry. Adultery was not intended in this statement[26] because adultery

---

[25] Muslim (*hadith* 1163)

[26] His statement "Adultery was not intended in this statement" is questionable, because the original meaning of *al-fahisha al-mubayyinah* is adultery. Al-Hafith Ibn Katheer said in his interpretation of the Allah's statement in chapter al-Nisa, verse 19 "إلا أن يأتين بفاحشة مبينة" meaning "Unless it is proven that they committed adultery", Ibn Mas'oud, Ibn 'Abbass, Sa'eed ibn al-Musayyab, Al-Sha'bee, Al-Hasan Al-Basree, Muhammad ibn Sireen, Sa'eed ibn Jubair, Mujahid, 'Ikrimah, Ataa Al-Kharasani, Al-Dhahak, Abu Qalabah, Abu Salih, As-Sidee, Zaid ibn Aslam, and Sa'eed ibn Abee Hilal alls said that it means adultery. This means that if she commits adultery, you have the right to retrieve the dowry which you gave her, and to pressure her until she returns it to you. Further, you can divorce her as Allah, the Most-High, says in chapter al-Baqarah,

و لا يحل لكم أن تأخذوا مما آتيتموهن شيئا إلا أن يخافا أن لا يقيما حدود الله

"It is not allowed that you (men) take any of the dowry that you have given them (your wives) unless they fear that they will not abide by the laws of Allah [giving the due rights to one another in marriage]." ... to the end of

49

is unlawful and is cause for the firm legal punishment [mandated in the *Shariah*].

The Prophet (may the most special blessings of Allah and peace be upon him) indeed said, "**Hit women lightly, without causing pain, if they disobey you concerning common rights (*ma'roof*).**" Then al-Qurtubi said, "Allah's statement, "فإن اطعنكم" means if they stop their transgression "فلا تبغوا عليهن سبيلا" meaning don't transgress upon their rights by saying or doing things that harm them. Herein, there is prohibition of wronging women, following the affirmation that men do have a rank over them, and they have been made responsible to establish the good etiquettes and dealings of women. It is also said that the meaning is: do not try and force them to love you because that is not something they have control over. His statement,

إن الله كان عليا كبيرا

means "Indeed Allah is the Most-High, the Superior" addresses husbands, ordering them to be compassionate and easy going with women; meaning, though you see yourselves stronger and more able than women [in many ways], keep in mind Allah's ultimate strength and ability. His power and ability are above all. Therefore, no man should deem himself superior to his wife because Allah is watching. Thus, the

---

the verse. Ibn Abbass, Al-Dhahak and 'Ikrimah said, "*al-fahishah al-mubayyinah*" is transgression (*nushuz*) and disobedience (*isyan*). As for Ibn Jarir, he held the position that it encompasses adultery, disobedience, transgression and bad-mouthing, as well as other actions. He means that all of these actions give license [to a husband] to pressure her until she returns the dowry to him or some of it and he then divorces her.

description in the verse of [Allah's] loftiness and superiority is extremely suitable.

This being the case, know [without doubt] that Allah, Mighty and Glorious, did not explicitly give an order to hit anywhere in His book except here and with the most severe legal punishments for particular crimes. Therefore, He thereby likened their disobedience to their husbands to major sins, and he turned the [correction of the] issue over to the husbands instead of the official leaders [and government], making it the responsibility of the husbands instead of judges, void of the need for witnesses or proof. This is a trust given by Allah, the Most-High, to men concerning [their] women.

Al-Mulahhab said, "Hitting women has only been permitted to address instances in which they prevent their husbands from having sexual intercourse with them."

Al-Hafith ibn Katheer said in his interpretation [of the Qur'an], "Iyas ibn Abdullah ibn Abu Thiyab reported, "The Prophet (may the most special blessings of Allah and peace be upon him) said,

لا تضربوا إماء الله

'Do not hit the female slaves of Allah'.[27]

So, Omar came (may Allah have mercy on him) to the Messenger of Allah (may the most special blessings of Allah

---

[27] *Sunan Abu Dawud* (hadith 2146); al-Albani graded it *sahih* (authentic)

and peace be upon him) and said, "The women have begun transgressing upon their husbands' rights, so the Messenger of Allah (may the most special blessings of Allah and peace be upon him) permitted that they be hit [lightly]. So, droves of women surrounded the family members of the Prophet complaining about their husbands. So, the Prophet said, 'Droves of women have surrounded Muhammad's family complaining about their husbands; those [men] are not the best of you." Reported by Abu Dawud, al-Nasaa'i, and Ibn Majah.

Further Clarification on The Wisdom and Legal Rulings Encapsulated in These Hadiths

In the *hadith* reported by Muslim, the Prophet (may the most special blessings of Allah and peace be upon him) clarified that the cause which permits hitting women [lightly] is when they allow someone their husbands do not like into their homes. This includes any man or woman who [a particular woman knows for sure that] her husband would dislike that they enter his home. Further, al-Imam al-Qurtubi understood from the *hadith* of al-Tirmithi that it is when adultery has clearly been committed that hitting a woman [lightly] is permitted, a hit which does not cause pain. Moreover, this hitting has been interpreted as being like hitting with a *siwak*, which is a [very] small, short [pencil-sized] twig from the *arak* and other such trees with which a man [traditionally] cleans his teeth. Moreover, this type of hitting has only been permitted to be a gesture symbolizing the correction of ill-behavior and as an expression of one's displeasure. In line with this is the *hadith* which emphasizes the command that women are to be well taken care of and treated in the best of manners. The word *a'wan* [in this *hadith*] is the plural of *a'niyah* which means prisoner, [signifying the fact that she is] committed solely to her husband and is unable to leave him; she does not leave home against his will and in this way, she resembles one in captivity who is unable to escape. Further, the Prophet (may the most special blessings of Allah and peace be upon him) taught that as long as a woman does not allow anyone her husband hates into their home, and as long as she does not avoid him [denying him sexual relations], or leave his home against his will, then he has no other rights over her. We understand from this that if a woman does commit one of these acts, and her man has hope that their relationship can be rectified; and he believes that in hitting her lightly in a manner which does not hurt, as detailed above, their relationship could possibly return to a good and healthy state, it is permitted for him to hit her [lightly] with the intention of rectifying their marriage ~ not with the intention of getting revenge. However, if he believes, due to his experience with her, that hitting her will not cause her to correct herself, but rather, will cause her to become even more obstinate and ultimately destroy her; and if he has no hope that they can live together in peace, it is not permitted that he hit her at all. He has the right, in such a case, to request that the dowry he gave be returned to him, and he should divorce her, which will be further addressed.

It is well-known that women are not all the same: some of them can be positively impacted by a [light] hit, while others would be destroyed by such a gesture. The aim of the Legislator [of these laws, Allah] is improving and rectifying [people and affairs] not destroying them. A wife [in many instances] could be young still needing the discipline of her parents, and an intelligent, rational man marries her. He thereby fulfills the role of her parents [in a sense], reprimanding and educating her in order to develop and cultivate her manners and etiquettes up until she has grown and matured mentally. This is the [type of] circumstance for which [light] hitting is allowed. This is keeping in mind that the Legislator (Allah) did not permit hitting unless [first] admonishing the woman and then refusing to have sexual intercourse with her has no positive impact on her ~ even though the cause for which hitting has been made permissible has been committed by the woman. The narration which is found in *Saheeh al-Bukhari* supports this understanding; the *hadith* in which the Prophet (may the most special blessings of Allah and peace be upon him) said,

ما بال احدكم يضرب امرأته ضرب الفحل, و لعله يضاجعها من ليلته

"What is the state [of illness] of the one amongst you who would hit his wife, like a horse is whipped, then have sexual intercourse with her that very same night."[28] ~ or it was something to that effect (the Prophetic *hadith*).

The Messenger of Allah (may the most special blessings of Allah and peace be upon) spoke the truth [concerning this, plain and clear]: how is it sensible that a man could hit his wife then hug her and kiss her? There is great contradiction in this since such hitting causes further distance [between spouses] and completely destroys love, which is the very soul of a peaceful, healthy marriage. Without such love, there is no good for either spouse in their being together. Rather, good ~ all of it ~ lies in them separating. This is because the very foundation of a blissful marriage is love and trust between husband and wife. So, when these two are lost, the rope which bonds husband and wife is severed, and each of the two

---

[28] Al Bukhari (*hadith* 6042)

becomes a torment and burden upon the other. Concerning the statement of al-Qurtubi "... and they must not anger them," this is from among those personal positions of his, and his own opinion ~ something [he personally] added [of his viewpoint] as an addition to that which the Prophet (may the most special blessings of Allah and peace be upon him) said. Allah did not permit that a man hit his wife every time she makes him angry. This is a grave error, and Muslims have the greatest model in their Prophet (may the most special blessings of Allah and peace be upon him). His wives made him angry so much so that he vowed not to be with them intimately for an entire month. However, he did not hit any one of them. They had asked him to provide more financial support which was above the lifestyle of simplicity that he wanted to lead. So, Allah ordered him to give them an ultimatum as is found in the chapter al-Ahzab. He did not hit even one of them. So, this is merely the error of a scholar. This *imam* fell into this error and may Allah forgive him. As for the statement of al-Qurtubi, "And the Prophet (may the most special blessings of Allah and peace be upon him) indeed said, 'Hit women lightly, in a manner that does not hurt, when they disobey you regarding an affair which is (*ma'roof*) commonly known as a basic right or standard of good behavior [in accordance with the *Sharia'h*].' This is the way he presented the narration, leaving it with no complete reference. He did not give its source. Neither did he mention its level of authenticity or weakness. Therefore, it is as if it is nonexistent. Further, in a case in which it were proven to be an authentic *hadith* of the Prophet (may the most special blessings of Allah and peace be upon him), disobedience must be interpreted according to the very clear explanations found in the authentic *hadiths* which have preceded; it is allowing people that he hates into his home, and refusing to be intimate with him. Once he has first admonished her and then refused to have sex with her, [he might choose to hit her lightly], if he believes this can help bring about rectification. This is the reason for which the condition of her disobedience is tied specifically to affairs described as being *ma'roof* (commonly known as a basic right or standard of good behavior in accordance with the *Shari'ah*). Concerning the statement of al-Qurtubi "Following the affirmation that men do have a rank over them," that which is intended concerning rank here is the position of leadership and bearing responsibility [for the family] and this fact has been eluded to previously. As for his statement, "and he turned the [correction of the] issue over to the husbands instead of the official leaders [and government], this means that if a woman does something which results in her husband being permitted to lightly hit her, from among the reasons previously mentioned, the man does not have to raise the affair to the leader [or government officials] ~ and this is what is intended by the expression *imam* ~ for someone [official] to give him permission to lightly hit her.

In the statement of al-Muhallab, a glorious scholar, "Hitting women lightly was only permitted to deal with their refusing to have sexual intercourse with their husband." *Al-mubadha'ah* is sexual intercourse. Therefore, this scholar limited the permissibility of lightly hitting a woman to instances in which she refuses to have sexual intercourse with her husband. That which is mentioned in the *hadith* concerning a woman allowing people that her husband hates into their home should be added here [to the reasons] and actions which resemble this [sort of obstinate behavior] that point to a woman's taking her husband's values and honor for granted.

Furthermore, based on our knowledge and experience, lightly hitting a woman who refuses to have sexual intercourse with her husband does not rectify the affair [or have a positive impact] unless the woman is very young or mentally immature. Hitting only pushes most women further away, causing the opposite of what is intended. So, instead of drawing her closer, he pushes her further away and the burning fire expands just as we witness [happening around us]. In the *hadith* of Abu Dawud, the Messenger of Allah (may the most special blessings of Allah and peace be upon him) forbade hitting women. So, women angered their husbands [even more]. The author of the book *Lisan [al-Arab]* said, "al-Asma'i said, 'this [women angering their husbands] means they rebelled, transgressed boundaries and became haughty with them. Therefore, you can see that this *hadith* is consistent with the previous *hadiths* in that hitting is not permissible except when there is *nushuz* (transgression). This being the case, after women had gone to the Prophet's (may the most special blessings of Allah and peace be upon him) house complaining about their husbands, he said concerning those who hit their wives,

ليس أولئك بخياركم

"Those [who do that] are not the best of you"[29].

Further, [he said] in the authentic *hadith*,

خيركم خيركم لأهله و أنا خيركم لأهلي

"The best of you is he who is the best to his family ~ and I am the best of you to my family."[30]

It is for this reason that there has been no report that the Prophet (may the most special blessings of Allah and peace be upon him) hit the wife of his who had transgressed. She was the daughter of al-Jaun whom he had married and when he drew near to her, she said, "I seek refuge with Allah from you." He, then, said to her, "Indeed you have sought refuge with One who can truly provide refuge. Go back to your family."[31] ~ reported by al-Bukhari. Therefore, the Prophetic tradition, as it relates to what the Prophet personally implemented, is that he abstained from hitting women even though it is permitted [in very specific instances]. Further, the Prophetic tradition from the aspect of what he has said concerning the issue can be found above in his statement (may the most special blessings and peace be upon him), **"Those [who do that] are not the best of you."** So, the best approach is to never hit women.

So, the three related affairs have been categorized: the type of hitting, its purpose, and its legality. Furthermore, the majority

---

[29] *Sunan Abu Dawud* (*hadith* 2146); al-Albani graded it *sahih* (authentic)

[30] *Sunan Ibn Majah* (*hadith* 1977); al-Albani graded it *sahih* (authentic)

[31] Al Bukhari (*hadith* 5255)

of Muslims who have been accustomed to hitting women are Bedouins of rural areas and the likes[32] who do not know these rules and limits. They, therefore, treat their women like animals transgressing the boundaries set by Allah, and they live in constant [marital] turmoil. So, their lives are not pleasant, nor do they have peace of mind. In the Sunan of Ibn Majah, it is reported that the Prophet (may the most special blessings of Allah and peace be upon him) said,

من سعادة المرء ان تكون له زوجة صالحة, إن نظر إليها سرته, و

إن أمرها أطاعته, و إن غاب عنها حفظه في نفسها و ماله

"Of the essential components of a man's overall happiness is a good woman: whenever he looks at her it makes him happy; whenever he orders her, she obeys him; and whenever he is absent, she protects him by protecting herself [from doing anything

---

[32] As for the ignorant people from among Moroccans and others, they indeed hit their women for the undeserving reasons in a manner which no one deserves except particular criminals. I once had a neighbor in Tangier in 1943. I heard him striking his wife, and I could hear the the stick hitting her body, and she would say ~ with every strike ~ "I wish for my destruction". My heart nearly tore apart out of empathy for her, but I had no power to rid her of the issue. I gathered from what he said that the cause for the discord was that there was not enough coal. She said, "I used it to light the fire. Do you think I sold it or ate it? Oh, how suitable was the saying of the poet, al-Hamasi who said,

رأيت رجالا يضربون نساءهم, فشلت يميني حين أضرب زينبا

"I have seen men hitting their women, may my right hand go limp were I to hit Zainab."

unbecoming of a good wife] and by safeguarding his wealth."[33]

This *hadīth* has been graded *hasan*. So, have a look ~ may Allah have mercy on you ~ at this *hadith* which is proof, through its tremendous wisdom, that this has come from the two lips of he who was given the amazing ability to speak with extraordinary wisdom and conciseness. He was given the ability to express profound meanings with unrivaled brevity. In this *hadith*, he has gathered the conditions which bring about marital bliss:

1. That a woman be beautiful in the eyes of the man
2. That she earnestly responds to his needs and does all that he wants her to do; and this specifically is the sign of deeply-rooted love
3. That he trusts her, and she trusts him. So, when he is not around for a long or short period, he can be at ease knowing that she will protect her honor and nobility and protect his wealth from being lost or wasted away.

Without these conditions, a marriage will never ever be blissful. Europeans claim that they have reached extreme marital bliss as a result of a potential husband spending lots of time with the proposed wife before the marital contract ~ spending time [alone] which causes doubts [about their chastity and nobility]. This can go on for years all the while they claim that each person gets to truly know the other, and

---

[33] Sunan Ibn Majah (*hadith* 1857); al-Albani graded it *da'eef* (unsound)

that each one is able to thoroughly study the character and nature of the other, resulting in a better chance of compatibility and long-term marital happiness. In reality, they know this is a false claim because neither husband or wife trusts the other [in these cases normally], not concerning the safeguard of honor or wealth; also due to the fact that the man cannot order his wife to do anything since obedience to him is not mandatory with them. So, the husband and wife are like two partners in business or a field of work. This is proof that the second condition, which is love, has been spoiled. Concerning the proof that intermingling before marriage does not enable either person to truly know the character of the other, it is that each person puts on a show for the other and exaggerates their feelings out of fear that their engagement will be spoiled. Almost no one reveals their true character until after marriage and examples of this are abundant. Once, in Bonn, Germany, an engaged couple remained engaged living together as a man lives with his wife for twenty years. Then, when they finally got married, they only stayed married for a year. The entire marriage was arguing, disagreements and animosity, ending in divorce.[34] Muslims of old, on the other hand, used to neglect the first condition preventing the proposing man and the woman to whom he is proposing from actually seeing each other before marriage. Doing this, they were actually opposing the authentic *hadith*, the statement of the Prophet (may the most special blessings of Allah and peace be upon him),

---

[34] The likes of this happens very often. It is a well-known common occurrence with them and this short book is not meant to showcase more than this one example.

"إذا أراد أحدكم أن يتزوج امرأة فلينظر إليها فإنه أحرى ان يؤدم بينهما"

"Whenever one of you wants to marry a woman, let him look at her; because, indeed, this increases the chances of their relationship lasting."[35]

This means that it increases the chances of them getting along. As for what is happening these days, they have indeed abandoned the *Shari'ah* of Allah ~ I mean most of them. They have followed in the footsteps of Europeans who they claim are their enemies because they have colonized them and raped [their lands]. So, they now intermingle before marriage with the women they propose to and whatever calamities and atrocities happen, they just happen.

تعسا لمن يشري الهدى بضلالة

كما فعلت فيما مضى عصبة السبت

و الله لا يهدي كيد الخائنين

Destruction to the one who sales guidance in
exchange for misguidance,
Just as the faction of the Sabbath did,
And Allah never guides the plot of the
treacherous.

---

[35] Sunan al-Tirmithi (*hadith* 1087); al-Albani graded it *sahih* (authentic)

Guidance of Islam Concerning Good Treatment of Women

Allah, the Most-High, said in the chapter al-Nisa, verse 19,

﴿ وَعَاشِرُوهُنَّ بِالْمَعْرُوفِ فَإِن كَرِهْتُمُوهُنَّ فَعَسَىٰ أَن تَكْرَهُواْ شَيْئًا وَيَجْعَلَ ٱللَّهُ فِيهِ خَيْرًا كَثِيرًا ﴿١٩﴾ ﴾

"And treat women with goodness and decency and if you happen to dislike them, then it may be that you dislike something in which Allah will place an abundance of good." [al-Nisa: 4:19]

The great memorizer, Ibn Kathir (may Allah have mercy on him) said in his explanation of this verse, "Concerning His, the Most-High's, statement,

و عاشروهن بالمعروف

And treat women with goodness and decency' it means speak with them in a good manner and be kind with them in your actions and mannerism as much as you can. Just as you like such treatment from her, reciprocate her with the same kind of treatment. It is just as Allah, the Most-High has said,

و لهن مثل الذي عليهن بالمعروف

'And just as men have rights over them, women have similar rights over men'. Further, the Prophet (may the most special blessings of Allah and peace be upon him) said,

خيركم خيركم لأهله و أنا خيركم لأهلي

"The best of you is he who is best to his family [in treatment] ~ and I am the best of you to my family."[36]

Of the core aspects of the Prophet's character (may the most special blessings of Allah and peace be upon him) was that he was beautiful in his treatment of his family, always smiling, playing with his family and showing tremendous compassion for them. He would give them graciously for their financial needs. He would make his wives laugh. He even used to race A'ishah, an expression of his tremendous love for her, the mother of the believers (may Allah have mercy on her). She said,

سابقني رسول الله فسبقته و ذلك قبل أن أحمل اللحم, ثم سابقته بعد ما حملت اللحم فسبقني فقال: هذه بتلك

'Race me, Messenger of Allah; so, I beat him, and that was before I gained some weight. Then, I raced him again after I had gained weight and he beat me. He said, 'This win for that one'.[37]

Sometimes, the Prophet would gather his wives in the home of the wife he would be staying with that night (may the most special blessings of Allah and peace be upon him). He would

---

[36] Sunan Ibn Majah (*hadith* 1977); al-Albani graded it *sahih* (authentic)

[37] Sunan Abu Dawud (*hadith* 2578); al-Albani graded it *sahih* (authentic)

eat dinner with them on some occasions. Then, each wife would go to her home. He used to sleep with each wife [when he was at her home] under the same blanket. He would remove his *rida* (upper garment) and sleep in his *izar* (lower/wrap worn by men). Once he had prayed the *isha* prayer, he would go into his house [for the night] and talk with his family for a while before sleeping. With this practice, he maintained a close and loving relationship with them (may the most special blessings of Allah and peace be upon him). Further, Allah said,

$$﴿ لَّقَدۡ كَانَ لَكُمۡ فِى رَسُولِ ٱللَّهِ أُسۡوَةٌ حَسَنَةٌ لِّمَن كَانَ يَرۡجُواْ ٱللَّهَ وَٱلۡيَوۡمَ ٱلۡأَخِرَ وَذَكَرَ ٱللَّهَ كَثِيرًا ﴿٢١﴾ ﴾$$

"There was, indeed, a tremendous example for you in the Messenger of Allah"[38] [al-Ahzab: 33:21]

---

[38] Concerning his statement, "Allah said, 'قد كان في رسول الله أسوة حسنة' **'There was, indeed, a tremendous example for you in the Messenger of Allah'**", the great scholar, Ibn Katheer (may Allah have mercy on him), implored all Muslims to follow in the footsteps of the Prophet (may the most special blessings of Allah and peace be upon him) in these noble characteristics with which he carried himself in his treatment of his wives. Therefore, it is mandatory that every Muslim man measure the way he lives with and treats his wives against this [noble] character. If he finds that his dealings are in accordance with it or close to it, he should be pleased that he will be rewarded greatly because he has followed [the way of the Prophet] and has been blessed to be guided upon the right way. Whereas, if he finds that his treatment of his wife is in opposition to the way of the Prophet, he should make repentance to Allah, the Most-High, and return at once to upright treatment of his family.

Al-Qurtubi said in his explanation of this verse, "The statement of the Most-High (Allah),

$$﴿ وَعَاشِرُوهُنَّ بِالْمَعْرُوفِ فَإِن كَرِهْتُمُوهُنَّ فَعَسَىٰ أَن تَكْرَهُوا۟ شَيْئًا وَيَجْعَلَ اللَّهُ فِيهِ خَيْرًا كَثِيرًا ﴾$$

"And treat women with goodness and decency and if you happen to dislike them, then it may be that you dislike something in which Allah will place an abundance of good."
[al-Nisa' 4:19]

This means treat them as Allah has commanded you to, living with them in kindness and good treatment. This statement is directed to all [men], since every man is either a husband or responsible for a female relative; though, husbands are the primary men intended here. This is similar to His, the Most-High's, statement,

$$﴿ فَإِمْسَاكٌ بِمَعْرُوفٍ ﴾$$

"So keep them, in kindness." [al-Baqarah 2:229]

This is fulfilling her rights regarding her dowry and financial needs, not frowning at her unless she is actually at fault. He must be kind in his speech with her, not harsh or hard, nor showing favoritism towards other wives. It should be a relationship in which they spend time with each other and live together in harmony. It is like the saying of Tarfah,[39]

---

[39] In Tarfah's statement, "شطت فإِنْ..." to the end of the poetic verse, al-nawa (النوى) means a far away distance, and shattat (شطت) means to go far

فلئن شطت نواها مرة

لعلى عهد حبيب معتشر

"Even when she goes too far [erring] here or there,
She is devoutly committed to her relationship with her beloved."

Herein, he used the word *habeeb* (حبيب) for plural [though it is generally for singular] just as the word *khaleet* (خليط). Further, the word *aa'sharah* (عاشره) [meaning to live in a close relationship] and *mu'aasharah* (معاشرة) [meaning living in a close relationship] and *ta'aashara* (تعاشر) [meaning he/they lived in a close relationship] with a people; and it is also said *i'tasharu* (اعتشروا) [meaning they lived together in a close relationship].

---

away. As for *mu'tashir* (معتشر), it means living in kindness and good treatment. He is saying that even if the home of your beloved is far away and it has become difficult to visit her, she is still committed to her relationship and love. The distance has not changed her commitment to her relationship nor has it altered her love. Furthermore, the usage of *fa'eel* (a nominal word scale in Arabic) for male and female, for singular and plural, is found in the speech of Arabs; rather, even in the Book of Allah, All-Mighty and Glorious, in chapter al-A'raf, verse 56, " ان رحمة الله قريب من المحسنين" "Indeed, the mercy of Allah is always nearby for doers of good." He also said, "و الملائكة بعد ذلك ظهير" "And the angels, all the while, are in full support [of the Prophet]." In addition, a poet once said, " يعادين من شيبه قد بدا, و هن صديق لمن لم يشب" "Women complain about his (their husbands') gray hair which has begun to appear, yet they do not mind being merely the girlfriends of those who have not yet grown gray hair."

T.N.: In the Arabic line of poetry above at the end of the footnote, the author gives another example of the noun form *fa'eel*, which is normally used for singular male, being used for plural female.

Therefore, Allah (highly exalted is He above all imperfections) mandated that women be treated well whenever someone commits to marrying them so that their connection and closeness can be [as] complete [as possible]. Indeed, it is best for one's soul [and spirit], and it brings about a more pleasing existence. This is mandatory upon the husband, not made mandatory due to a court order [but because Allah has ordered it].[40]

Some scholars said, "This is for a man to exert great effort in treating his wife well just as she does for him." Yahya ibn 'Abd al-Rahman al-Hanthali said, "I came to Muhammad ibn al-Hanafiyah and he came out to me in a red, cloak-like garment. His beard was dripping with expensive, scented oil. So, I said,

---

[40] Concerning his statement, "... not mandatory due to a court order", he means that the good treatment which is due to women has been made mandatory upon husbands by Allah. Furthermore, a woman cannot [really] complain to a judge if her husband is falling short in this aspect since there is really no way by which the judge could truly know the authenticity of her claim. Allah has made this the responsibility of husbands; if they do it, he rewards them. On the other hand, if they abandon it, they are held accountable by Allah, since He is the one who will punish them. However, some scholars of *fiqh* (Islamic jurisprudence) do not agree with this viewpoint. Rather, they hold that a wife should be provided accommodations near upright people. If they witness mistreatment, a judge then forces the husband to divorce her. However, the prior viewpoint seems to be the most sound, because if a man frowns in his wife's face, or his wife speaks to him yet he does not answer her, or if he does other such actions or [utters unjust, bad] words, which neighbors would not [normally] be able to witness, how then would the woman be able to prove what happened? So, a woman who has the bad fortune of being married to a husband of bad character and who treats her badly and is difficult to live with, she must exercise patience and look forward to her reward from Allah. If she is unable, she must raise her issue to a judge and let him know that she has come to hate her husband. She must request a divorce just as the wife of Thabit ibn Qays ibn Shamas did.

'What is this?' He said, 'My wife covered me with this garment and put fragrance on me; and, indeed, they desire from us the same kind of treatment we desire from them." Ibn 'Abbas (may Allah have mercy on him) said, "I absolutely love to dress well and to look good for my wife just as she loves to dress well and look good for me." This is consistent with what we have already mentioned. Ibn 'Attiyah said, "And for the meaning of the verse [in chapter al-Nisa' above], the statement of the Prophet (may the most special blessings of Allah and peace be upon him) must be referenced, "فاستمتع بها و فيها عوج" "Then, enjoy being with her, though there will always be an aspect of her [nature and behavior] which has 'iwaj (i.e. literally, a curve; meaning a difficulty)." This means that you must not treat her badly due to a deficiency[41] in her, from which disagreement

---

[41] Muslim reported in the Book of Marriage in his Sahih, with his chain of narrators to Abu Hurairah; he said, "The Messenger of Allah (may the most special blessings of Allah and peace be upon him) said,

من كان يؤمن بالله و اليوم الآخر, فإذا شهد أمرا فليتكلم بخير, أو ليسكت, ة استوصوا بالنساء خيرا, فإن المرأة خلقت من ضلع, و إن أعوج شيء في الضلع أعلاه, إن ذهبت تقيمه كسرته و إن تركته لم يزل أعوج, استوصوا بالنساء خيرا

"Whoever believes in Allah and the Last Day, whenever he witnesses something, he should say good [beneficial] things or be quiet. Furthermore, be good to women, because indeed women were created from a rib, and the most curved part of a rib is the uppermost part. If you try to straighten it, you will break it whereas, if you leave it, it will remain curved. So, be good to women," and in another narration after his statement (may peace be upon him) "كسرته" "you will break it," he said " و كسرها طلاقها" "... and breaking her is divorce."

So, in this noble *hadith* there is emphasis on the advice of treating women well and being patient with their deficiency because this is their nature in general and it is not out of ill intent. Further, whoever wants to straighten

arises and severe marital discord occurs. This is the cause of *al-khul'ah*.

Our scholars have used His, the Most-High's, statement,

$$﴿ وَعَاشِرُوهُنَّ بِٱلْمَعْرُوفِ ﴾$$

"And treat women with goodness and decency."

as proof that if one helper [or housemaid] is not sufficient for a woman, that he must facilitate help for her according to her needs. Such as the daughter of the Caliph, or of the King and the likes, all of whom need more than one helper [or housemaid]. This would be [considered] good, decent treatment [for this particular scenario]. Abu Hanifah and al-Shafi'i said, "More than one helper [or housemaid] is not binding upon him. It suffices that she take care of herself and there is no woman in the world except that one helper [or housemaid] suffices for her. Just as is the case with a warrior who has several horses. He can only use one horse, because it is not possible for him to fight on more than one horse. Our scholars have said, "This is incorrect, because daughters of

___

out the makeup [of a woman] until she is perfect, he has sought the impossible. In addition, living together is all about patience, forgiving, and forbearance in dealings towards men or women. Concerning this, oh how great was the saying of the poet who said, " اذا انت لم تشرب مرارا على القذى ظمئت "و أي الناس تصفو مشاربه, و من ذا الذي ترضي سجاياه كلها كفى المرء نبلا أن تعد معايبه " "If you do not drink regularly from liquid which does have particles in it, you will go thirsty ~ and whose drinks are completely pure? Further, who is he that is pleased with all of his characteristics? That a man count [and recognize] his shortcomings is a noteworthy act of nobility."

kings who have many helpers [and housemaids], one maid is not enough for them. This is because she needs her clothes washed and her bed made and the many other tasks which one helper is not able to handle, and this is clear. ~ and Allah knows best.

Summarized and Concise Legal Affairs of The Khul'ah

﴿ سُبْحَـٰنَكَ لَا عِلْمَ لَنَآ إِلَّا مَا عَلَّمْتَنَآ إِنَّكَ أَنتَ ٱلْعَلِيمُ ٱلْحَكِيمُ ﴾

"You are so highly exalted above all imperfections. We have no knowledge other than what you have taught us. Indeed, you are the All-Knowing, the Most-Wise."
[al-Baqarah 2:32]

Respected readers, men and women, know that Islam is the religion of intellect and freedom bounded by justice. Know that there is no exclusion and no superiority. It is the religion of justice and equality in rights and responsibilities, firmly repudiating all oppression and mistreatment and caste systems. Therefore, it is not at all allowed in the true *Shari'ah* of Allah, which has not been altered or changed, to force a woman to stay with a man, ever. A woman has the same rights as a man in this affair except that the divorce is put in the hands of the man due to the fact that he is the leader carrying the relative responsibilities which the *Shari'ah* and nature demand of him ~ as long as he does not transgress the boundaries set by Allah. With regards to the wife, she can officially leave whoever she does not like at any time and in any situation ~ whenever she has grown to hate her husband. This may be due to bad character, or unattractive physical features. All she has to do is raise her issue to an upright judge [who implements the true guidance of the *Shari'ah*]. She should present the dowry that he had given her at which point it is mandatory that the judge order the husband to accept the dowry back. The husband must then accept the dowry back and separate from her immediately.

As for the case in which the husband, the judge, or both of them are ignorant of the *Shari'ah* of Allah, so one of them or both of them force the woman to stay [as if she is] a prisoner with a man she does not love or trust, such a ruling [and action] is incorrect and invalid. It is something that Allah has not allowed, and the explanation and proof concerning this follows.

First, allow me to define *al-khul'ah*. Al-Hafith ibn Hajr in al-Fath said, "*Al-khul'ah*, with a *damma* (vowel sound of 'o') over the first letter of the word and a *sukoon* (consonant sound with absence of a vowel) over the second letter, in language, means for a woman to leave [her husband] in exchange for an amount of money. The word is taken from the expression '*khal'u al-thobe*' (to remove one's garment), because the woman, symbolically, is like the clothing [or covering] of the man. The *damma* (Arabic vowel sounding like 'o' of English) in this noun[42] serves to differentiate between the physical meaning

---

[42] Al-Hafith's statement, "The *damma* (vowel sound of 'o') in this noun serves to differentiate between the physical meaning and the symbolic meaning" means that the *khul'ah* between spouses each of whom are like a garment (of protection) for the other. Allah, the Most-High, says in chapter al-Baqarah, "هن لباس لكم و أنتم لباس لهن" "They are a garment for you, and you are a garment for them." [al-Baqarah: 187].

With a *damma* (Arabic vowel sounding like "o" of English) on the letter "خ" and it is at the beginning of the word (خلع), *khul'u* here is symbolic since

[such as removing clothes] and the symbolic meaning [which is when a woman leaves her husband].

---

neither of the two spouses is taking off clothes. As for *khal'u*, with a *fatha* (Arabic vowel sounding like "a" of English) for its "خ" (first letter).

The First Khul'ah to Happen
Among Arabs Before Islam

Ibn Durayd said in his work "Amali", "Indeed, the first *khul'ah* which occurred in the world (he means in the Arab world) is when Aamir ibn al-Tharb married his daughter to his brother's son, Aamir ibn al-Harth ibn al-Tharb. When she first went to him, she avoided him. So, he complained about this to her father. He replied, 'I will not cause you to have left your family and your money. Indeed, I grant the *khul'ah* for you from her by returning to you that which you gave her (the dowry).'" He said, "So, scholars have asserted that this was the first *khul'ah* among Arabs."

Muhammad Taqi al-Deen said:

From this story, we know that the woman in the "days of ignorance" was a respected, honored woman who held her own affairs in her hand. Not her father, nor tradition or any other guardian could force her to be the partner of a man she hated. Islam only increased her in her freedom, honor and respect and you will all see the evidence of that.

The First Khul'ah that Happened in Islam

Al-Hafith said, "Al-Bazzar reported in the *hadith* of 'Omar that he said, 'The first woman to get a *khul'ah* in Islam was Habibah bint Sahl. She was married to Thabit ibn Qays." ~ and he mentioned the rest of the *hadith*.

A Glimpse at Some of the Hadiths on the Khul'ah

The first is the *hadith* of the wife of Thabit ibn Qays ibn Shammas al-Ansari. The narrators of the *hadith* differed concerning her name; some said "Jamilah", others said "Habibah", and yet others said other names. Al-Bukhari reported, with his chain of narrators back to ibn 'Abbas, "That the wife of Thabit ibn Qays came to the Prophet (may the most special blessings of Allah and peace be upon him) and said, 'O Messenger of Allah, I am not angry with Thabit ibn Qays regarding his character or his [practice of the] religion, but I would hate to commit [an act] of disbelief after having become Muslim.' So, the Prophet (may the most special blessings of Allah and peace be upon him) said, 'Will you return his garden to him?' She replied, 'Yes.' The Messenger of Allah (may the most special blessings of Allah and peace be upon him) said [to Thabit], 'Accept the garden [from her] and divorce her once.'"

Also, in a narration reported by al-Bukhari [there is the following wording], "Will you return his garden to him?" She said, "Yes." So, he ordered him to divorce her.

Muhammad Taqi al-Deen said:

His statement and his order for him to divorce her renders false the statement of those who say that the command in his statement (may the most special blessings of Allah and peace be upon him), "Accept the garden and divorce her," is an order of guidance or rectification, not an order which mandates the affair. This is a strange understanding. How can a woman hate her husband with the severest level of hatred, to the point at which she fears that if she were forced to remain with him, she would disbelieve in Allah? She raised her issue to the judge which was the Prophet (may the most special blessings of Allah and peace be upon him). He commanded that the [return of the] garden, which was her dowry, be accepted. He said to him (Thabit ibn Qays), "Divorce her." Then, all of this would be considered simple guidance and rectification and not binding. It is not even fathomable that it would be permissible for Thabit ibn Qays to say to the Prophet (may the most special blessings of Allah and peace be upon him), "No. I do not accept [the garden] and I will not divorce her." This is what the statement of those who say that the command here is merely for guidance and rectification necessitates. Then, there was another narration, clearly an order. So, there remained no room for interpreters [to interpret otherwise].

Imam Malik's Narration of this Hadith

Imam Malik said in his Muwatta, "From Yahya ibn Sa'id, from Amrah bint 'Abd al-Rahman ibn Sa'id ibn Zararah who informed him about Habibah bint Sahl al-Ansari, that she was married to Thabit ibn Qays ibn Shammas. The Messenger of Allah (may the most special blessings of Allah and peace be upon him) was leaving out for *al-subh* (fajr prayer) and found Habibah bint Sahl at his door in the early morning darkness. The Prophet (may the most special blessings of Allah and peace be upon him) said, "Who is this?" She replied, "I am Habibah bint Sahl." So, he said, "What is the matter?" So, she replied, "Not me; not Thabit ibn Qays for a husband." So, when Thabit ibn Qays came, the Messenger of Allah (may the most special blessings of Allah and peace be upon him) said to him, "This is Habibah bint Sahl. She has mentioned [concerning your marital issues] that which Allah has decreed she would mention. Habibah said, "Oh Messenger of Allah. Everything that he has given me I still have." So, the Messenger of Allah (may the most special blessings of Allah and peace be upon him) said [to Thabit], "Take it from her." So, he (Thabit) took it back from her, and she went to abide with her family.[43]

In the narration of Malik, there is a very useful addition which is that [we learn that] from the severity of her hatred for her husband, she did not wait until the Prophet (may the most special blessings of Allah and peace be upon him) had finished

---

[43] Sunan Abu Dawud (*hadith* 2227); al-Albani graded it *sahih* (authentic).

praying *al-subh*. She stood at the door of his home to expedite her separation from the one she hated (her husband). We also find in this narration that she went to abide with her family meaning she left her home as of that moment. She lived with her family and did not spend the *'iddah* (waiting period for the *khul'ah* ~ one month) in Thabit's house.

The Second Hadith: Al-Hafith Ibn Kathir said in his *Tafsir*, the Imam Abu 'Abdullah ibn Battah said, and mentioned his chain of narrators back to Ibn 'Abbas, "That Jalilah bint Salul came to the Prophet (may the most special blessings of Allah and peace be upon him) and said, 'By Allah, I am not angry with Thabit ibn Qays regarding a religious or character issue; however, I hate [that one falls into] disbelief [while] in Islam. My hatred for him is unbearable.' So, the Prophet (may the most special blessings of Allah and peace be upon him) asked her, 'Will you return his garden to him?' She said, 'Yes.' So, the Prophet (may the most special blessings of Allah and peace be upon him) ordered him to take that which was sensible and not to go beyond that.'" After mentioning the chain of narrations for this *hadith*, Ibn Kathir said, "It has a good, sound chain of narrations.[44]

The Third Hadith: Al-Hafith Ibn Kathir said, "And Ibn Jarir said, having mentioned his chain of narrators back to 'Abdullah ibn Rabah. He reported from Jamilah bint 'Abdullah ibn Ubay ibn Salul that she was married to Thabit ibn Qays and she transgressed against his rights. So, the Prophet (may the most special blessings of Allah and peace be

---

[44] Sunan Ibn Majah (*hadith* 2056); al-Albani graded it *sahih* (authentic).

upon him) sent for her and said to her, "Jamilah, what do you hate about Thabit?" She replied, "I do not hate his practice of the religion or his character. The only issue is that I hate his ugly face." So, he said to her, "Will you return his garden to him?" She replied, "Yes." So, she returned his garden to him, and he separated them.[45]

The Fourth Hadith: Al-Hafith Ibn Kathir said, Ibn Majah said, mentioning his chain of narrators back to 'Amr ibn Shu'ayb from his father and grandfather, "Habibah bint Sahl was married to Thabit ibn Qays ibn Shammas, and he was an ugly man. So, she said, "O Messenger of Allah. By Allah, if it were not for my fear of Allah, I would spit in his face whenever came into my presence." So, the Prophet (may the most special blessings of Allah and peace be upon him) asked her, "Will you return his garden to him?" She replied, "Yes." He said, "So, the Messenger of Allah (may the most special blessings of Allah and peace be upon him) separated them."[46]

The Fifth Hadith: Al-Qurtubi said in his *Tafsir*, "Ikrimah reported from Ibn 'Abbas that he said, 'The first to do a *khul'ah* in Islam was the sister of 'Abdullah ibn Ubay. She went to the Prophet (may the most special blessings of Allah and peace be upon him) and said, 'O Messenger of Allah. My head and his will never come together. Indeed, I raised a side of my tent [to see him] and saw that he had come in a group. He was the blackest of them, the shortest of them, and the one with the ugliest face.' So, the Prophet (may the most special

---

[45] Al Bukhari (*hadith* 5276)
[46] Al Bukhari (*hadith* 5276)

blessings of Allah and peace be upon him) asked her, 'Will you return his garden to him?' She replied, 'Yes, and Allah willing, I can give more.' So, he separated them."[47] Al-Qurtubi said, "This *hadith* is a foundational (piece of) evidence on the topic of the *khul'ah*, and the vast majority of the scholars of Islamic jurisprudence adhere to [principles of] this evidence.

.

---

[47] From these *hadiths* and others, we come to know that the reason for which Habibah hated her husband, the profound lecturer of the *Ansar*, Thabit ibn Qays ibn Shammas. Further, some narrators reported that he hit her and broke her hand. This [narration] is not authentic, because the *hadiths* all coincide on two points which negate the soundness of this narration. The first point is that she said, "I do not hate him for his character or his practice of the religion." If he had hit her, even with a *siwak* stick [as small as they are], or if he had not hit her but said an evil word to her which had angered her and hurt her, she would not have testified to the goodness of his character while seeking to divorce him. Rather, she would have considered her reason for leaving him valid and mentioned it to the Prophet (may the most special blessings of Allah and peace be upon him), that he had hit her and broke her hand. She would not have concealed that.

The second is that she mentioned the reason for which she hated him, which was that his face was ugly and that if it were not for the fear of Allah, she would have spit in his face whenever he came into her presence.

Interpretation of the Qur'anic Khul'ah Verse

Know that the scholars, may Allah have mercy on them, interpreted the *khul'ah* verse with the best of explanations. They mentioned the legal affairs that it addresses with the supporting evidence. I will choose two explanations from among the many, the interpretations of two glorious *imams*. One of them follows the approach of the *kufiyoon* and the second of them follows the approach of the *hijaziyyun*. Become familiar with the concepts followed by each group and their points of view. Al-Imam Abu Bakr Ahmad ibn 'Ali al-Jassas said in his book, "The Legal Rulings of the Qur'an," in summary, "Allah, the Most-High, said,

$$﴿ وَلَا يَحِلُّ لَكُمْ أَن تَأْخُذُوا۟ مِمَّآ ءَاتَيْتُمُوهُنَّ شَيْـًٔا إِلَّآ أَن يَخَافَآ أَلَّا يُقِيمَا حُدُودَ ٱللَّهِ فَإِنْ خِفْتُمْ أَلَّا يُقِيمَا حُدُودَ ٱللَّهِ فَلَا جُنَاحَ عَلَيْهِمَا فِيمَا ٱفْتَدَتْ بِهِۦ ۗ تِلْكَ حُدُودُ ٱللَّهِ فَلَا تَعْتَدُوهَا وَمَن يَتَعَدَّ حُدُودَ ٱللَّهِ ﴾$$

"It is not allowed that you take any of the dowry that you have given to them unless they fear that they will not abide by the laws of Allah [giving the due rights to one another in marriage]."
[al-Baqarah 2:229]

Here, He restrains the husband with this verse from taking away anything which he had given her, except with the

84

condition that was mentioned.[48] Furthermore, it is understood from this that it is not permitted that he take

---

[48] Regarding his statement, "... except with the condition mentioned" I will mention here a nice story that one of the brothers from Najd told me because of the related benefits which it entails. I hope that those from Najd who are extreme in their concern with lineage do not get angry with me, or anyone else. Some brothers from Najd told me that a man [can be for example] from the *qabaliyun*, and these are those who know the details of their lineage, meaning they know the tribes of the Arabs from which they all hold that they are from. Further, this is considered the second rank of those who have noble lineage with the people of Najd and those who follow their way among the tribes of Iraq and Hijaz. This is because, indeed, they hold that tribes are of three categories, and there is looseness and variation with the particular names used for each. The rank of the *shaikhs*: these are the princes like Ali Saud, Ali Khalifah in Bahrain, Ali Sabah in Kuwait and others. This is the highest rank. The *qabaliyun*, which were mentioned, are the second rank, and they are, in actuality, one [with the first] rank. There is no actual difference between them in lineage; they share one. It may be just that the *shaikhs* seek to raise their status above average *qabaliyun* when it comes to marriage. They refuse to marry other than the daughters of princes, and this is rare; however, they diligently seek to [at least] marry their daughters to the sons of other *shaikhs*. As for the third rank, they call them the *khudairiyoon*. Some have said that this name has been altered from its original *hudairiyoon*, meaning the people of modernity and city life, those whose lineage is unknown. The scholars among them might even call them *mawali* (freed slaves). So, concerning these *khudayriyyun*, the *qabaliyun*, not to mention the *shaikhs*, hold that they are not fit to be in-laws and, therefore, they do not marry from among them; nor do they marry those under their guardianship to them. They go to great extremes concerning this affair to the extent that if a *khudayri* marries a *qabali* woman correctly according to *Shari'ah*, her relatives might even kill him. They may even kill her *wali* who married him to her. On the other hand, if they are weak and unable to kill him, they divorce her relatives, such as her sister or her aunt and so on [if any of their family members are married into her family]. This is because the *wali* who married his female relative to a *khudayri* person has given up his noble lineage, for himself and his immediate family. He is counted among the *khudayriyyun* from that point on. The same goes for a *qabali* man who marries a *khudayriyyah* (*khudayri* woman); he will be threatened with death

until he divorces her. We have, indeed, witnessed incidents of this nature, though this is not the place to mention them. Furthermore, if a *qabali* argues with a *khudayri*, the *qabali* says to the *khudayri* "Be quiet you white slave!" Also, when a strange person comes to their land, even when they know his lineage, they treat him as a *khudayri*, even if he were from the family of the Prophet (may the most special blessings of Allah and peace be upon him). They excuse themselves saying that they are unable to verify his lineage with certainty, and that if they could verify his lineage by any means, they would, no doubt, marry him [to one of their female relatives]. Moreover, it is obligatory that a *qabali* abstain from working in any occupation which is considered lowly such as the occupation of cupping or cutting hair for example. If he works in such occupations, he loses his lineage and honor. Based on these details, the story is built. So, a *qabali* married a *qabaliyah* (*qabali* woman) without having looked at her [or having seen her] beforehand. He, thereafter, found that she was ugly, and he had already spent an abundant amount of money on their marriage. So, he lost a lot and the whole earth felt as if it were closing in on him. In his eyes, the world became dark because he would not be able to obtain the money it would take for him to marry another woman. So, he dwelled in misery, sad. Then, some of his friends came and found him in this state of pity. So, he (one of the friends) said to him, "I have a solution for you, my brother. I will explain it to you and with it, you will be able to retrieve all you spent on this woman." So, he said, "Tell me at once brother. May Allah reward you with good." So, he said, "Go to such-and-such barber and sit with him for a long time. Learn his skill, even if you only learn it a little. Then, open a barber shop. When the relatives of your wife see you in this state, they will become extremely angry. They will tell you that you must either abandon this trade or divorce our daughter. So, tell them to return the dowry, and you will divorce her. They will surely do that." So, he did what his friend told him to do. He learned [cutting hair] for a month, and then bought barber tools and opened a barber shop. He started cutting people's hair. The relatives of his wife came and called him bad names and were severely enraged. So, he told them that this kind of work is permissible in the *Shari'ah* and he will not abandon it. So, they ransomed their daughter (his wife) from him. When he received the money, he abandoned the barber shop.

There are two other ranks [concerning lineage], rather three. Ranks which are far lower than the *khudayriyyun* [in "rank"] to the extent that others will not even eat with them or drink with them, such as those who are spread throughout India, and they are the tribes of "*Munaim*" and "*al-Salbah*" and

anything from her which he had not given her; even though the above-mentioned [verse] is concerning particular money or wealth he may have given her. This is just as is the case with the statement of the Most-High,

$$\{ \text{فَلَا تَقُل لَّهُمَآ أُفٍّ} \}$$

"And do not even say *uff* (an expression of disgust) to them (parents)." [al-Isra' 17:23]

Which is proof that worse actions like hitting and reviling them are prohibited as well. Also, there is the verse,

$$\{ \text{إِلَّآ أَن يَخَافَآ أَلَّا يُقِيمَا حُدُودَ ٱللَّهِ} \}$$

"... unless they fear that they will not abide by the laws of Allah [giving the due rights to one another in marriage]."
[al-Baqarah 2:229]

Tawus said concerning this verse, "This is referring to the rules which are made mandatory on each [the husband and wife] concerning their marital life and companionship. Al-Qasim

---

"*al-Kawawilah*". This last rank is the one that is referred to as "*al-fajr*" in Egypt. They are found in Europe and are despised for that. Further, I have written a piece in German called [that which means] "Ranks Among Arabs". I expounded therein on the excellence of Islam and its erasing these ranks, and on how Arabs returned to these ranks after becoming weak in Islam.

This piece was distributed in the German Magazine called, "Deyer Islam" and the European lovers of Arabic and Arabic culture considered it very valuable since they were ignorant of these issues.

87

ibn Muhammad had a similar statement. The scholars of language say, "الا ان يخافا" "**... unless they fear...**" means "unless they think". Al-Fira, may Allah have mercy on him, recited a poem to Abu Muhjan al-Thaqafi saying,

إذا مت فادفني إلى جنب كرمة

تروي عظامي بعد موتي عروقها

و لا تدفني بالعراء فإنني

أخاف إذا ما مت أن لا أذوقها

When I die, bury me next to someone noble,
That her sweat could nourish my bones once I am dead,
Do not bury me in a barren, exposed land,
I fear that once I am dead, I would not then taste it.[49]

---

[49] His statement "أذوقها" "taste it" is with "*raf'u*" (an Arabic grammar form) due to the article "أن" (pronounced "an") which is "*nasibah*" (another Arabic grammar form) after the word "أخاف" (pronounced "*akhaf*" = I fear) which means here "بما أظن" (I think; as far as I see). Further, it is well known that after "أظن", the grammatical changes it normally necessitates can be implemented or left off. If left them off; it is considered a less complex form of the phrase, as opposed to its more complex form.
Ibn Malik said in his "*Alfiyah*",

لا بعد علم و التي من بعد ظن   ''و بلن انصبه وكي كذا بان

تخفيفها من ان فهو مطرد   فانصب بها و الرفع صحح واعتقد

"And with "*lan*" I change the grammatical form of a word to "*mansub*" and with "*kay*" and likewise with "an", but not after [words which have the meaning of] "knowledge" nor after [words that have the meaning of] "thought".
So, apply the grammatical case of "*nasb*" to them (changing words to this grammatical form) or implement "*raf'u*" and know that it is correct and consider it,
Lightening the complexity [of the grammar] from that which is used with "an" since it is not needed [in this case]

And yet another poet said,

أتاني كلام عن نصيب يقوله

و ما خقت يا سلام أنك عائبي

Some information has reached me from a trusted source,
And I never feared, O Salam, that you would speak ill of
me.

"I never feared here" means "I didn't think."

This fear that the laws of Allah would be abandoned has two
aspects: It is either that one of them has very bad character, or
both of them. Hence, this would lead to the abandonment of
Allah's laws regarding the marital rights He has mandated for
each spouse [from the other]. Further, in the statement of the
Most-High,

﴿ وَلَهُنَّ مِثْلُ ٱلَّذِى عَلَيْهِنَّ بِٱلْمَعْرُوفِ ﴾

"And they have rights due to them similar to those
which others have over them." [al-Baqarah 2:228]

Or it may be that one of the spouses hates the other, making
it difficult for one to live in kindness, good treatment, and
putting up a front. This, in turn, would lead to one disobeying
the commands of Allah, neglecting the marital rights which
each is responsible for upholding. Moreover, if one of these

two cases occurs, and they fear that they would abandon the laws set by Allah for each, the *khul'ah* can ensue.

Furthermore, Jabir al-Ju'fi reported from 'Abdullah ibn Yahya from 'Ali (may Allah make his face of the most honorable) that he said, "There are particular words which if a woman says them, it is allowed that a man take back the dowry: if she says, "I will not obey anything you order me to do;" "I will not fulfill a sworn promise," or "I will not clean myself from *janabah* (the state after menstrual cycle, or after having sex, etc.).

Al-Bukhari said in his *Sahih* in the chapter of *al-khul'ah*, "Tawus said, "الا أن يخافا أن لا يقيما حدود الله" "... unless they fear that they will not abide by the laws of Allah [giving the due rights to one another in marriage]" is referring to the rights due to each person from their spouse as it relates to their marital life and companionship. He did not say as the foolish say, that there is no issue until the wife says, "I will not clean myself from *janabah*."

Muhammad Taqi al-Deen said:

If you were to say, "How could this be a narration attributed to 'Ali while Tawus considered it of the sayings of the foolish; and further, al-Bukhari reported it and kept quiet about the comment?" The answer is that this narration is not authentically traced back to 'Ali.

Al-Hafith ibn Hajr said in "al-Fath", "Indeed, Ibn Abu Shaybah reported it from 'Ali with an extremely weak chain of narrators, meaning it is *da'if* (an unauthentic narration). Al-Hafith mentioned in "al-Fath" from a group of *tabi'in* that they said something similar. He hinted therein that what they intended was to give an example. They did not intend by this that a *khul'u* could not ensue unless the wife said such a phrase. Rather, once good marital treatment is not fulfilled and affairs become bad between the two, the *khul'u* is allowed even without such expressions [being uttered by the wife].

The meaning of "I will not fulfill a sworn promise" is "If you swear that I will do something [or else], I will never do it." This is [done by some wives] to ensure that her husband will become among those who break their promises. Also, if he were to try and initiate sexual intercourse with her, she would refuse; there would then be no *janabah*, and therefore, no *ightisal* (special shower for cleaning oneself after sexual intercourse). Further, when a woman's hatred of her husband reaches this level, there is no treatment for them nor any cure other than the *khul'u*. This requires that she give back the dowry that he had given her, and he must then let her go.

Al-Qurtubi's Interpretation of the Verse

The Imam, Abu 'Abdullah Muhammad ibn Ahmad al-Ansari, said, in summary, "The statement of the Most-High, " فإن خفتم ألا يقيما" "So, if you fear that you will not uphold..." means that they will not uphold "حدود الله" "... the laws of Allah." This is referring to the obligations on each spouse including being a companion, being pleasant to live with. Furthermore, this verse addresses the authorities and arbitrators concerning these issues, even if they are not judges [of law]. Moreover, a woman's "not upholding the laws of Allah" is her making light of the rights of her husband, as well as her poor level of obedience to him. Ibn Abbas, Malik ibn Anas, and the vast majority of the scholars of jurisprudence hold this position.

Al-Hasan ibn Abu al-Hasan and a group of people with him said, "If a woman says, 'I will not obey anything you order me to do, and I will not clean myself from *janabah*, nor will I fulfill any swear that you make,' the *khul'u* is permissible." Further, Ata' ibn Abu Rabah said, "The *khul'u* is permissible as well as taking the dowry back when a woman says to her husband, 'Indeed, I hate you, I do not love you' and similar statements.[50]

﴿ فَلَا جُنَاحَ عَلَيْهِمَا فِيمَا ٱفْتَدَتْ بِهِۦٓ ﴾

---

[50] In this, along with the preceding arguments, there is proof that the love a man has for his woman has no bearing here if the woman hates him.

"Then, there is no blame on them if she ransoms herself [paying an amount back to her husband to get out of the situation]." [al-Baqarah 2:229]

Thereafter, he mentioned the *hadith* of Thabit's wife which we have presented. Then, he said, "She used to hate him with a passion." Whereas, he used to love her tremendously. So, the Messenger of Allah (may the most special blessings of Allah and peace be upon him) separated them by way of the *khul'u*.

Differences Amongst the Salaf, and Other Scholars of Jurisprudence from Various Lands, on What is Allowed to Be Taken in the Khul'u

Al-Jassas said in "*al-Ahkam*", "It is reported that 'Ali (may Allah be pleased with him) hated [the idea of a man] taking more than he gave her. Further, this is the position of Sa'id ibn al-Musayyib, al-Hassan, Tawus, and Sa'id ibn Jubayr. It is reported that 'Omar, 'Othman, Ibn 'Omar, Ibn 'Abbas, Mujahid, Ibrahim, and al-Hasan all said that it is permissible for him to release her in a *khul'u* in exchange for more than he had given her even if it were [as little as the value of] her hair tie." Whereas, Abu Hanifah, Zafar, Abu Yusuf and Muhammad all said, "If the transgression is on her part, it is allowed that he take back that which he had given her but not more than that amount. However, if the transgression is on his part, it is not allowed that he take anything back from her, though if he did, it would have to be by way of an official legal ruling." Ibn Shibrimah said, "Divorce is allowed so long as there is no injustice that results from it, so if it would result in injustice, it is not permissible [in such cases]." Ibn Wahab said that Malik said, "When it is known that her husband has harmed her, made her life difficult and oppressed her, she must be given a divorce, and her money must be returned to her." In addition, Ibn al-Qasim reported that Malik said that it is allowed in a *khul'u* for a man to take more than he had given his wife, that is permissible for him. Though, if the transgression was on his part, he is allowed to take whatever she offers in the *khul'u* as long as she is pleased with that, and as long as he is not harming her by way of that." Layth said something similar to this. Al-Thawri said, "When the *khul'u* is from her, there is no problem that he receives [an amount] of money from her. However, if it (divorce) is initiated by him, it is not permissible for him to take anything from her.

Muhammad Taqi al-Deen said:

This means that when she is requesting the *khul'u* and divorce, her husband is allowed to receive an amount of money from her. On the other hand, if he is the one who hates her and wants to divorce, it is not then allowed that he receive any money from her. Furthermore, this position has also been transmitted from many scholars, yet those we have mentioned suffice.

The Viewpoint of Not Taking Any Increase is the Soundest Position

Bear in mind that the scholars differed concerning whether or not the husband can receive more for a *khul'u* than the dowry he had given to his wife. One group from among the *Salaf* (foremost scholars of early Islamic history) and latter scholars said that it is allowed for her to seek to free herself [from the marriage] with whatever amount they both agree upon, whether that be a large or small amount. Al-Bukhari said in his *Sahih*, "And 'Othman allowed the *khul'u* for less than [the amount of] a hair tie she uses for her head."

Al-Hafith ibn Hajr said in "al-Fath", "Al-'Iqas (عقاص = a hair tie) with *kasra* (an Arabic grammatical form) of the first letter of the word, lightening of the ق (the second letter of the word), and the last letter is a ص with no punctuation. It is the plural form of the word "'uqsah" (عقصة), and it is used to tie the hair of one's head after gathering it together. Concerning the saying of Othman that I mentioned, it was presented with its fully connected chain of narrators in "Amali Abu al-Qasim ibn Bishran." Something similar was also narrated from Ibrahim al-Nakha'i, and Mujahid except that he said the man can take even the hair tie from the head of the woman requesting a *khul'u*. Something similar was also narrated from Qabidhah ibn Thuwayb. Then, he said, "Ibn Battal said, 'The vast majority of scholars hold the position that it is allowed for a man to receive for a *khul'u* more than he had given the woman.'" Malik said, "I have not seen anyone, who is worthy of being taken as an example, that does not allow that; yet, it is not consistent with the higher standards of good character."

Then, Al-Hafith said, "Imam Ahmad said, 'Indeed, the *khul'u* is an abrogation of the marriage.' He said in another narration, "And, indeed, she is not allowed to marry any other man until three of her menstrual cycles have passed.'[51] So, he saw no necessary connection between the *khul'u* being an abrogation and there being a shorter waiting period. Moreover, he used this as evidence to support [his position] that the amount given [for the *khul'u*] must not differ from the exact amount the man gave the woman, or the same value. He bases this on the saying [of the Prophet], "Will you return his garden to him?" In the narration of Sa'id ibn Qatadah from 'Ikrimah from Ibn 'Abbas in the last *hadith* of the related chapter for Ibn Majah and al-Bayhaqi, "So, he ordered him to receive [an amount] from her and not to take more [than what he had given her]." Further, Ibn Jurayj reported this from Ata' with a chain which was *mursal* (missing the companion of the Prophet, who actually heard the *hadith* from the Prophet). There is also a narration that Ibn al-Mubarak and 'Abd al-Wahhab [reported] from him, "As for any excess amount, then no." Ibn al-Mubarak added from Malik, and in a narration from al-Thawri, "And he hated [the idea] of taking more from her than he had given her." Al-Bayhaqi mentioned all of this. Also, in the *mursal* of Abu al-Zubayr reported by al-Daruqutni and al-Bayhaqi, "Will you return to him the garden which he gave you?" She said, "Yes, and more." The Prophet, (may the

---

[51] The scholars have differed on the *'iddah* (waiting period) of the woman who has been granted a *khul'u*. As for those who say that the *khul'u* is the same as *talaq* (divorce initiated by the husband), they mandate that the woman observe a waiting period of three "quru" meaning menstrual cycles. Conversely, those who say that it is an abrogation of the marriage and not the same as a common divorce [initiated by the husband] made her waiting period only one menstrual cycle. Al-Hafith has reported a position of Ahmed, which is invalid, that he considers it (the *khul'u*) an abrogation yet holds that the woman must observe a three-menstrual-cycle waiting period.

most special blessings of Allah and peace be upon him) said, "As for any excess amount, then no, but just the garden." She said, "Yes." So, he received his money and let her move on ~ and the men of this chain of narrators are all trustworthy. Then he said, "Abd al-Razzaq reported from 'Ali, "Do not take from her more than what you gave her." Tawus, al-Zuhri, and 'Ata reported something similar. This is also the position of Abu Hanifah, Ahmed, and Ishaq. Further, Isma'il ibn Ishaq reported that Maymun ibn Mahran said, "Whoever takes more than what he gave her has not 'let her go in kindness.'[52]" Contrary to this, there is the report from 'Abd al-Razzaq, with an authentic chain of narrators, from Sa'id ibn al-Musayyib who said, "I do not like that he takes all of that which he gave her. Let him leave something [of it] with her."

Imam Abu Muhammad 'Abdullah ibn Ahmad ibn Qudamah said in "Al-Mugni" the following, "It is not preferred that he receive more than the amount he gave her." This statement is proof of the soundness of a khul'u in which more than the dowry is returned to the husband, and that if they agree upon an amount for the khul'u, it is sound [and valid]. Further, this is the position of most scholars." Then, he went on to mention arguments and evidence similar to that which has preceded herein concerning the permissibility of a man taking back more than he gave her. Then he said, "With this [clearly] established, it is [still] not preferred that a man take back more than he gave her. Ibn al-Musayyib, al-Hasan, al-Sha'bi, al-

---

[52] T.N.: This refers to the verse in the Qur'an which orders that a man has a choice, after having pronounced divorce twice, to either keep his wife upholding the known standards of goodness or let her go in kindness. Allah says, "فأمساك بمعروف أو تسريح بإحسان" "So, choose either holding on to them upholding the known standards of goodness [in your treatment of them] or letting them go in kindness." [al-Baqarah 2:229]

Hakam, Hammad, Ishaq, and Abu Ubayd held this position, so if he does [take more], it is allowed, though it is disliked.

In addition, it was reported from Ata that the Prophet (may the most special blessings of Allah and peace be upon him) disliked [the idea] that he would take from a woman seeking a *khul'u* more than he had given her [for her dowry]. Abu Hafs reported this, with his chain of narrators, and the ruling is very straight forward. Hence, we combine the [implications] of the verse and reports and we say: the verse is proof that it is permissible whereas the prohibition of taking back an excess amount [in the reports] is for the purpose of expressing that it is disliked ~ and Allah knows best.

Muhammad Taqi al-Din said:

Abu Bakr al-Jassas said, "After that which has preceded, He (i.e., Allah) gave permission in this verse for the man to take [back an amount] when the two spouses fear that they will neglect the laws set by Allah. This is referring to the information we have presented about when a woman hates her husband, and when she behaves in a bad way, or when such problems stem from both of them. In such cases, it is allowed for a man to take back the dowry he gave her, yet he should not take more than that. The apparent ruling necessitates the permissibility of taking it all back while the point about an excess amount has to do more specifically with the *Sunnah*." This usage of the evidence is correct since there is no clear evidence in the verse which permits taking more than the amount of the dowry. The statement of the Most-High,

﴿ فَلَا جُنَاحَ عَلَيْهِمَا فِيمَا ٱفْتَدَتْ بِهِۦ ﴾

"So, there is no blame on them if she ransoms herself [paying an amount back to her husband to get out of the situation]." [al-Baqarah 2:229]

This means that there is no harm if the man takes back that which he had given the woman, and there is no harm in what the woman gives her husband. Furthermore, it is well known that the word "ما" (pronounced "ma") is from among a group of words [in Arabic] which connote generalization; therefore, it includes the amount of the dowry and could refer to less than that amount, as well as more than that amount. The reports from the *Sunnah* that have been presented have served to give more specifics [concerning this issue]. The Prophet (may the most special blessings of Allah and peace be upon him) unambiguously discouraged taking an excess amount and clarified that it is disliked. Further, the Imam Ibn Qudamah [even] held that considering that the hatred of it is merely to discourage is a position about which one should have doubt. This is because the foundational principle concerning things that are hated in the Book and *Sunnah* is that it connotes [that the hated act is] unlawful.

The collection of *hadiths* in which there is forbiddance of taking an excess amount provide ample proof for the prohibition of taking any excess amount, and nothing opposing it has proven to be sound. Malik said that taking an excess amount is not consistent with the higher standards of good character. In addition, Maymun ibn Mahran said, "Whoever takes more than he had given, has [by way of that action] not let her go in kindness." Indeed, Allah, the Most-High says,

$$﴿ فَإِمْسَاكُ بِمَعْرُوفٍ أَوْ تَسْرِيحُ بِإِحْسَنٍ ﴾$$

"So, [choose either] holding on to them upholding the known standards of goodness [in your treatment of them] or letting them go in kindness." [al-Baqarah 2:229]

Further, allowing men to take an excess amount could entice them to trap women in the relationship. Allah says in chapter al-Nisa', verse 19,

$$﴿ يَـٰٓأَيُّهَا ٱلَّذِينَ ءَامَنُوا۟ لَا يَحِلُّ لَكُمْ أَن تَرِثُوا۟ ٱلنِّسَآءَ كَرْهًا ۖ وَلَا تَعْضُلُوهُنَّ لِتَذْهَبُوا۟ بِبَعْضِ مَآ ءَاتَيْتُمُوهُنَّ إِلَّآ أَن يَأْتِينَ بِفَـٰحِشَةٍ مُّبَيِّنَةٍ ﴾$$

"O believers. You are not allowed to inherit women [taking them as wives] against their will, and do not seek to trap them in marriage in order to take back some of what you have given them unless it is proven that they have committed adultery." [al-Nisa' 4:19]

Al-Hafith ibn Kathir said, "This means do not make their lives difficult in order to force them to give back the dowry, or some of it; nor can you take away any right of hers which is due to her from you, or anything of the sort, in an oppressive manner in order to harm her."

Muhammad Taqi al-Din al-Hilali said:

One might say, "If transgression in a marriage (*nushuz*) is on the part of the wife, while the husband loves her, why is it not allowed for him to punish her by taking an excess amount beyond the amount of the dowry he gave her even if that were the amount of a hair tie, as payback for the hatred she has for him. The answer is that love and hatred is in the hands of Allah, the Most-High. He is the One who controls hearts, so a woman should not be punished for something that she does not control. Just as is the case if a man has two or more wives, and he loves one of the two ~ or one of them ~ more, Allah, the Most-High, does not punish him for that as long as he treats them fairly in his spending and providing shelter for them, and treats them as well as he can. Allah, the Most-High, says in chapter al-Nisa', verse 129,

﴿ وَلَن تَسْتَطِيعُوٓا۟ أَن تَعْدِلُوا۟ بَيْنَ ٱلنِّسَآءِ وَلَوْ حَرَصْتُمْ فَلَا تَمِيلُوا۟ كُلَّ ٱلْمَيْلِ فَتَذَرُوهَا كَٱلْمُعَلَّقَةِ وَإِن تُصْلِحُوا۟ وَتَتَّقُوا۟ فَإِنَّ ٱللَّهَ كَانَ غَفُورًا رَّحِيمًا ﴿١٢٩﴾ ﴾

"You will not be able to be just with them, even if you tried your best. Therefore, do not lean fully towards one of them leaving others like a hanging object. Yet, if you work to establish goodness and have deep regard for Allah, indeed, Allah is Oft-Forgiving, Most-Merciful."

[al-Nisa' 4:129]

﴿ وَإِن يَتَفَرَّقَا يُغْنِ ٱللَّهُ كُلًّا مِّن سَعَتِهِۦ وَكَانَ ٱللَّهُ وَٰسِعًا حَكِيمًا ﴿١٣٠﴾ ﴾

"And if they divorce, Allah will enrich each one of them from his endless abundance. Allah is All-Encompassing and Most-Wise." [al-Nisa' 4:130]

Al-Hafith ibn Kathir said in his Qur'anic interpretation, "His statement, "You will not be able to be just with them, even if you tried your best" means that you will not be able, O people, to make every single thing equal between women. Indeed, even when things are apparently divided evenly, a night for a night, there must necessarily be some difference when it comes to love, passion and sexual intercourse, just as Ibn 'Abbas said. Further, Imam Ahmad and the authors of the *Sunan* reported that A'ishah said, "The Messenger of Allah (may the most special blessings of Allah and peace be upon him) used to divide things among his wives justly and then say 'O Allah. This is how I have divided the things which I have control over. Please, do not blame me for that which I have no control over" meaning the heart.[53]

---

[53] Sunan Abu Dawud (*hadith* 2134); al-Albani graded it *da'if* (unsound).

Condemnation of Requesting the Khul'u Without Due Cause

Know, may Allah bless you and I to love all that the Messenger taught (may the most special blessings of Allah and peace be upon him), and to follow him and all that he made law, in every small and large affair, that it is not permitted for a woman to request the *khul'u* unless it is necessary. Likewise, it is not permissible that she be like those women who marry and divorce fleetingly, as is mentioned in a *hadith*.

"Indeed, Allah does not like those men and women who marry fleetingly." This narration was reported by al-Tabarani in "*al-Awsat*" from Ubadah ibn al-Samit, and al-Suyuti graded as *hasan* (a good, authentic grade for a *hadith*). Al-Haythami said, "There is a narrator in this chain of narrators who was not named. As for the rest of the chain, it is *hasan* [good and sound]. Al-Tabarani also reported it from Abu Musa al-Ash'ari, connected all the way back to the Prophet, that he said, 'I do not like those who marry fleetingly, men be they or women.'" Further, al-Daylami reported from Abu Hurairah alone with the utterance, "Marry, and do not divorce [quickly with no just cause], because, indeed, Allah does not like those who marry fleetingly." There is also the version of al-Haythami from Abu Musa that the Prophet (may the most special blessings of Allah and peace be upon him) said, "Do not divorce women unless you have doubt [about their loyalty]. Indeed, Allah Glorious and Most-High, does not like men and women who marry fleetingly." Al-Tabarani reported this in "*Al-Kabir*."

Those men who marry fleetingly are those who marry women to fulfill their sexual desires for the moment then they draw them along a bit, then divorce them. They then seek out other women. Women who marry fleetingly do the same. This is because Allah called good marital treatment "His laws", and he said that whoever transgresses those laws, they are wrongdoers. Moreover, marrying solely for temporal lust is a light form of [the illegal] *mut'ah*[54] [marriage]. Therefore, a man and a woman should only marry one another with sincere intentions to live in goodness until death separates them. Then, if circumstances which call for a divorce come about, and they are unable to uphold the laws set by Allah, divorce is allowed, though it is the most hated affair which is permitted[55]. Abu Dawud reported this from Ibn Majah from the *hadith* of Ibn 'Omar. Also, Ahmed and al-Tirmithi reported from Thawban (may Allah have mercy on him) that he said, "The Messenger of Allah (may the most special blessings of Allah and peace be upon him) said, 'Any woman who asked her husband for a divorce without just cause, the fragrance of Paradise is rendered illegal for her.' He also said, 'Women who do *khul'ahs* [unjustly] are hypocrites.'"

Muhammad Taqi al-Din said:

From this, it is known that it is not allowed for a woman to request the *khul'u* unless she sees in her man physical features

---

[54] T.N.: *Mut'ah* is a marriage for which the man and woman to be married agree upon a fixed period for the marriage, after which the marriage will end. This type of marriage has been ruled illegal in Islam.

[55] T.N.: The *hadith* which mentions this is graded weak as the scholars have made clear. However, some of the scholars say that the meaning is relevant. Shaykh Salih al-Fawzan has even said that the meaning is correct since divorce separates the family and he mentioned various other difficulties which divorce entails. He says in his book "Important Reminders on Affairs Which Concern Believing Women", "It (divorce) should only be sought when it is absolutely necessary. For it to be enacted without just cause is *makruh* (a permissible but hated affair)." [see "Important Reminders on Affairs Which Concern Believing Women", pg. 97, by al-Fawzan]

or character flaws which cause her to hate him, and when she knows that she is unable to live in good treatment and kindness.

Beneficial Point

In the information I transmitted herein from al-Hafith ibn Hajar, he mentioned that Imam Ahmad was of those who forbade taking an amount in excess of the amount of the dowry in the *khul'u*; however, the statements of Ibn Qudamah would seem to prove that he is among those who hold that it is allowed. This happens often: foremost scholars (*hufath*) who compile works of broad Islamic Jurisprudence report a position of one of the major *imams* [of the past] who are blindly followed [by many], while the scholars of that *imam's* school of thought report [a position] contrary to what the prior reported. Which position should be given precedence? As far as I see, the report of the foremost scholars takes precedence because these foremost scholars seek out the chains of narration [studying them in depth]. Whereas, indeed, blind followers may find two or more reports from their *imam* on one topic. They sometimes grade one of the reports as more sound and correct than the others ~ and Allah knows best.

Glossary

Ijazah: is the traditional Islamic system by which a teacher vouches and certifies that his student has studied and thoroughly grasped specific lessons or knowledge from him (i.e. *Qur'an*, *hadith*, etc.)

Nushuz: transgression

Hadith: prophetic narration

Hadith hasan sahih: authentic grade of prophetic narrations

Siwak: a small stick, about the size of a pencil, used traditionally by Muslims for cleaning one's teeth

Ma'ruf: actions and statements that are basic rights and standards of good behavior as legislated in the *Shari'ah*.

Rida: upper garment

Izar: lower wrap worn by men

Wali: Guardian who is responsible for marrying a woman to man

Janabah: ritual state in which one cannot perform prayer and specific acts of worship until one has performed *ightisal*[56] after one has had sexual intercourse

Ightisal: a special shower for cleaning oneself after sexual intercourse

---

[56] *Ightisal* is a special shower for cleaning oneself after sexual intercourse.

Made in the USA
Middletown, DE
14 March 2022